# MACHETE MOMENTS

## A Turnaround Manager: From Burned Out at Fifty-Four to Turned On for the Next Eighteen Years

### DOUG OTTO

iUniverse LLC
Bloomington

MACHETE MOMENTS
A TURNAROUND MANAGER: FROM BURNED OUT AT FIFTY-FOUR
TO TURNED ON FOR THE NEXT EIGHTEEN YEARS

iUniverse books may be ordered through booksellers or by contacting:

iUniverse
1663 Liberty Drive
Bloomington, IN 47403
www.iuniverse.com
1-800-Authors (1-800-288-4677)

Because of the dynamic nature of the Internet, any web addresses or links contained in this book may have changed since publication and may no longer be valid. The views expressed in this work are solely those of the author and do not necessarily reflect the views of the publisher, and the publisher hereby disclaims any responsibility for them.

Any people depicted in stock imagery provided by Thinkstock are models, and such images are being used for illustrative purposes only.

Certain stock imagery © Thinkstock.

ISBN: 978-1-4759-9630-2 (sc)
ISBN: 978-1-4759-9632-6 (hc)
ISBN: 978-1-4759-9631-9 (e)

Library of Congress Control Number: 2013911289

Printed in the United States of America.

iUniverse rev. date: 7/2/2013

# CONTENTS

To Carolyn who showed me what love means

To Greg, Cindy, Mike, and Betsy who gave
me countless reasons to be proud

To Lauren, Alison, Caroline, Meaghan, Patrick,
Cameron, Nolan, Mallory, Annabel, and Ashlyn
who have brought immeasurable joy to the autumn of my years

# MACHETE MOMENTS

A Turnaround Manager: From Burned Out at Fifty-Four
to Turned On for the Next Eighteen Years

--------------------------------------------------- I.

# THE BURNOUT

I am Joseph Paul Camarte. In 1995, I was a burned out business leader. After seventeen years as a plant manager and a chief operating officer in two manufacturing companies, I was clinically depressed. The rational side of my mind told me that I had a wonderful family, a home, abundant friends, and could play golf and tennis at least at a mediocre level. What could possibly drive me to this level of distress?

This is my story, but it could apply to any one of thousands of us who, after our fiftieth birthday, have needed a major change in our careers. The reasons driving the need vary. Some are suffering serious burnout, as I was. Others have been victims of downsizing or an unwanted transfer to another city. Some have decided, on their own, to seek work with less pressure and/or more meaning. Still others have been hit with a strong feeling of wanderlust. The reason doesn't matter. I would not presume to write a how-to manual for success in management. I think if I just share my experiences in both for-profit manufacturing and non-profit human services and demonstrate how I made the transition from one to the other, there might be a good chance that as you read, you will say, "That's me" or "I want that to be me."

The names of most people, places, and organizations have been changed to protect the privacy of those who have been a part of my life, but the episodes are based on real occurrences.

In 1995, I looked in the mirror. My manufacturing career had been successful and exciting. I was well known and respected in some circles as a crisis management specialist having led four turnarounds and a startup. I had been reasonably well paid, although I was far from wealthy. My wife, Kate, and I were each other's best friends. We were healthy, faithful, and still in love. Our four kids were doing remarkably well in their own lives. Three were through college and were supporting themselves while our baby was about to enter college. None of them had any serious problems. We had friends in our adopted hometown of Vienna, Indiana, where we had been since 1969. Vienna is in Sierra County in the southern half of the state. The population of the county is about 70,000 people, half of whom lived in our small city with the other half residing in the surrounding rural areas. It was a great place for kids to grow up—great parks, good schools, little crime. I had a nearly perfect life. And yet, I was depressed to the point of considering suicide. Where had it gone wrong?

The answer is that there was no specific moment things started downhill. It was what seemed like an inevitable crash based on my own feeling of insecurity. That included an inability to appreciate the success I had achieved because it was never enough. My accomplishments were recognized as outstanding, but I was nagged by the thought that the results should have been better, and I couldn't handle that.

Despite those feelings, I strongly deny that I am a perfectionist. In fact, I rail against that characteristic in others. I contend that, in most cases, the energy it takes to get from 95% perfect to 100% is wasted and leads to inefficient use of one's time. Open heart surgery and the manufacturing of airplane parts are exceptions to that theory.

At the point when my mood had hit bottom, a friend in Vienna came to me with what seemed to be an absurd proposition. He knew that I was suffering, although he was not aware of the degree. The presidency of the United Way in our county had been open for six-months, and no acceptable candidate had been discovered. I had led the annual fund raising campaign as a volunteer several years earlier and had been on the board of directors, but I certainly had never considered turning pro. The friend suggested that due to my senior management experience, the board might be willing to pay me off the chart for a United Way our size. Even then, I would be making half of what I had been making in manufacturing.

At the same time, I had an offer to become vice-president of operations for the U. S. division of a Japanese owned company. It was located in the same industrial park as my then employer. Nothing else in my life would have had to change. My immediate assignment would have been to lead a turnaround as I had three times before. The job would have paid what I had been making plus a new car every other year.

On the surface, it appeared to be a no-brainer which job to choose. Why would anyone in his right mind take a job for half the money he could make elsewhere? Except, I knew I was burned out. And I had no knowledge of the Japanese culture. I would have had to adjust to a whole new way of doing things including making multiple trips every year to Japan. Kate finally made the decision easy. One evening at dinner she proclaimed, "I want you alive and home, rather than suicidal and travelling around the world."

"Do you honestly not care about the reduced income?" I asked.

She reassured me, adding, "It helps that neither of us is materialistic. We don't chase the biggest home or the fanciest car, so we really don't need that much."

At 54, I totally changed careers from for-profit manufacturing to non-profit human services. I went from the monthly pressure of a balance sheet and operating statement to a leadership role among those whose mission it was to figure out how our community could best help people in need. I have made three great decisions in my life—(1) Marrying Kate, (2) Changing careers, and (3) Having my knees replaced.

Throughout my career in both for-profit and non-profit work, I have considered myself the luckiest man on the face of the earth since Lou Gehrig. (Kate tells me that if you have to explain them, you shouldn't use them, but I don't want this perfect metaphor to be wasted because you are too young to understand. On July 4, 1939, a dying Lou Gehrig told a crowd of 62,000 gathered to honor him at Yankee Stadium, "Today I consider myself the luckiest man on the face of the earth." His speech was immortalized in the 1942 Warner Brothers film *Pride of the Yankees* starring Gary Cooper as Gehrig.)

I believe that, at many junctures in my life, good luck might have been at least as big a factor as any intelligence or skill I may have possessed. When I'm tempted to get too full of myself, I try to remember that. However, I also believe that a person who works hard, listens, and is committed tends to experience more than his share of good luck.

# MY MANUFACTURING CAREER—PART ONE

## A Lucky Move

It was the late sixties. I had started in the business world applying my accounting degree. I quickly realized that I didn't enjoy this field because it stifled my creative and leadership abilities. It was boring, and frankly, I wasn't very good at it. However, in the sixties and seventies, companies and employees were loyal to each other and careers tended to remain on a straight path.

My first job out of school was as a staff accountant with what was then known as a Big Eight national CPA firm. I remember clearly the two moments when I realized that public accounting wasn't for me.

In 1965, I had been on the job a little over a year. Until then, accounting firms had pretty much restricted themselves to auditing and the preparation of tax returns. The managing partner of our office called a staff meeting to announce that the firm was going enter a new realm of business called management consulting. He shared the firm's plan to broaden its services to include assisting clients in developing and implementing strategic plans. The next day, I went to him to express interest in being a part of the new direction. His reply was blunt and was delivered without emotion. "Joe, what could you possibly imagine that anyone would want to consult you about?" He had me there. I shrunk back to my desk in the bull pen that housed the rest of the auditors, where I would remain for the balance of my brief public accounting career.

The second moment came a few weeks later and was more subtle but equally meaningful. It was the custom of the firm to place its accountants in various country clubs, city clubs, and other prestigious places where potential clients gathered. The firm picked up the tab for the dues and all business related expenses. That same partner called me to his office, and I thought, "Oh boy, I wonder which club he's going to put me in?" I had my golf clubs ready to go. In that same cold tone I remembered so well from my management consulting request, he offered to pay my dues to the downtown YMCA. I was pretty sure that I wasn't exactly on the fast track.

Two other accounting jobs with companies in the area proved to be no more fulfilling. As the last of my three jobs was winding down, I wandered into the office of a job search firm on a Saturday morning. As I was filling out the required forms, a middle-aged man came into the office. He said he was the controller of a manufacturing division of a Fortune 500 company in Indiana, and he was looking for an accountant with three years of experience who wouldn't demand too much money. I spoke up to say that he had just described me. We talked for about fifteen minutes, and he made me an offer, which I immediately accepted. I never did finish the paperwork, and he had no more discussions with the agency. I don't know if they collected a fee. I know that I didn't pay anything. Lou Gehrig had smiled on me big time!

The offer required me to pack up my family, and move to Indiana. In 1969, at age 28, Kate and I and our two young children moved from Columbus, Ohio, to Vienna, Indiana, so that I could begin an accounting job with the Kane Power Industries plant located there. This would be my fourth job and fourth residence in six years. I had to make this work, or potential employers would label me as an irresponsible drifter. At the time, I could not have denied the accuracy of that conclusion.

I then spent seven years kicking around in various accounting positions at Kane before escaping from the bean-counter strait-jacket around my career and gravitating to manufacturing operations. After a year in the role of manufacturing manager, I was promoted to plant manager of the Vienna plant, one of the company's many factories around the country.

At 37, I had become the youngest person ever to have been made plant manager in the history of Kane Power. Today it seems as though fast trackers are being appointed to that position almost out of college.

This was the first of several can't-lose opportunities I would be handed over the course of my career. When thinking about approaching a turnaround situation, I always recall the wisdom of an old Bobby Bare song, *When You Ain't Got Nothin', You Ain't Got Nothin' to Lose.*

# My Rookie Year

I had been at the Vienna plant I was to manage for eight years, including the seven spent in accounting. The plant had just come off a violent 5-month strike. During the strike, one of my responsibilities as manufacturing manager was to lead a skeleton crew to be on the inside when we knew there was going to be violence on the picket line. Our group became known among the non-striking employees as Joe's G. I.'s. There were those among us who had a good enough relationship with a few of the less militant strikers that we were warned when those times were coming. At least, we could answer urgent calls from customers, protect the computer, document the picket line activities on video tape, and communicate with the police. On days when the picket line was less threatening, salaried and non-exempt employees were invited to come in and work in the factory to produce emergency orders.

As the strike grew longer, the inside crew had been shot at, replacement workers had been followed to their homes and beaten, and cars of non-union employees trying to get onto the property had been rolled over with the drivers inside. When the strike was over, everyone on both sides of labor and management was angry.

Joe's G. I.'s spent much of our time in the front lobby of the office area. This was our war room. Here was where we made videotapes of the picket line activities. One of my most vivid memories occurred when the strike was about three months old. The front wall of the lobby was made up of three large glass windows from floor to ceiling. The G. I.'s were eating dinner one night shortly after dark. One of the more enthusiastic strikers climbed the chain link fence surrounding the property, performed a low crawl across fifty yards of lawn, and bashed out one of the windows out with a baseball bat. Glass flew through the lobby like shrapnel from a land mine. Two of our guys were cut—one needing emergency room treatment.

One of the concessions in the settlement was that the company would drop the charges against fourteen union members who had been arrested for violence during the strike. In addition, they would be reinstated as employees, and no disciplinary action would be imposed. I was furious at the decision by top management and didn't much care who knew it. I and others had literally risked our lives to save the plant, and we felt betrayed with what we saw as a management cave-in. That was when I got my first lesson in the concept of the greater good. I got a call from the Kane CEO in Philadelphia. He told me that he understood my feelings and that he was personally very appreciative of what our team on site had done. He also let me know that if the strike had run two more weeks, top management had already decided that the plant would be closed. Even when the strike ended, the opinions of senior management had been split as to whether to close it or give it one more chance with a new guy as plant manager. The next day, I got word that I was promoted to that position.

I thought long and hard about "the greater good." For decades, when left alone in the night with my thoughts, I have agonized over whether I had sold out in not only accepting management's decision but also in gaining personally from it? Those of us who had been through the battles all wanted to see those fourteen men punished. They had committed criminal acts and had endangered our personal well-being and our jobs. However, had I sulked away, the plant probably would have been closed, and my job and 400 others would have been lost. The ripple effect would have been felt throughout the community because Vienna would have lost one of its largest employers. Vengeance can be a great motivator, but it rarely leads to productive decisions. Fortunately, I learned quickly to swallow that desire in favor of the greater good. Should I be ashamed of that rationalization? Late at night, I'm still not quite certain.

About two months into the new job, I was called to corporate headquarters in Philadelphia to meet with Kane's executive vice-president/chief operating officer. He was a good old boy named Robert E Rutledge, who was so entrenched in southern living that he commuted every week from Savannah to Philadelphia. He proudly went by Robert E to all who knew him. Like Harry S Truman, E was his middle name. It was not an initial, and it stood for nothing.

I was ushered into Robert E's huge office. It had all the trappings one might expect of the egomaniac he was reputed to be. It covered about 2,000 square feet and contained what I estimated to be upwards of $100,000 worth of furniture and carpet. There were shelves full of trophies. On the walls were framed diplomas, both earned and honorary, patents, and a half-dozen wild animal heads, which I suspected he had killed with his bare hands.

Robert E arrived after he was certain that I was seated so that I could get the full effect of the grandeur of his entrance. No handshake was offered. Instead, he slowly went to his desk chair, seated himself, and stared at me without blinking for what seemed like ten minutes. Actually, it was probably twenty seconds, but it was long enough to make me extremely uncomfortable as I tried to return his gaze without looking away.

Without ever calling me by name, Robert E, in his extreme southern drawl, opened with, "What are you gonna do about that fuckin' mess out there in Indiana?" I started to answer that I was going to make some changes in the assembly line and shift some personnel. Robert E interrupted. "Yoou don't understaand. Yoou're tryin' to op-err-ate with a scalpel, and I'm tellin' you to use a Goddamn machete." That was the end of the meeting. Again without a handshake, a good luck, a good bye, or a go to hell, Robert E left the room. After the shock had started to wear off, I went to the outer office and asked his secretary if she knew if the meeting was over. She answered matter-of-factly, "Oh yes. In fact, your meeting lasted longer than many of Robert E's one-on-one meetings."

I can't stress strongly enough what a tremendous effect that meeting, especially Robert E's machete metaphor, had on the rest of my career. In order to fully embrace his term, I had to first give it a clear definition. What did it mean to me? I decided that a *machete moment* would be the successful implementation of an idea that those with less vision would see as too radical to consider—an action that I was convinced was the right path and would push forward in the face of opposition. I don't mean that I would not listen to well thought out logical arguments, but the knee-jerk reactions of naysayers and the cowardice of fools would not destroy my resolve.

On the way home from Philly, I tried to think of ways I could use Robert E's mandate to save the plant and my job. I landed upon the realization that, if I were to succeed, I had to regain the trust and support of the union work force.

I returned to my rather modest office. It contained furniture worth a few hundred dollars and sports photos along with cheap posters of John Belushi and Abbott and Costello on the walls. There, I began to research ways to heal the flaming resentment between labor and management. These were the pre-Google days, so research was more arduous than it would be today. The day after I got back in the office, a brochure came in the mail about something called a gain-sharing plan. Here's Lou Gehrig again. There was going to be a two-day seminar in Houston in two weeks. I knew only a little from the ad, but it was enough to induce me buy a plane ticket to Houston.

The issue with the union was strictly money. The hourly work force made 35% less than the big company in town, Denard, Inc. Denard's world headquarters was located in Vienna, and it had several manufacturing operations here. It was a multi-billion dollar company in the seventies when there weren't many of those around. In addition, another Fortune 500 company, Munsey Industries, was also headquartered along with two plants in Vienna. Munsey didn't pay at the same level as Denard, but their pay scale was considerably higher than Kane's. First Denard, and then Munsey, had their pick of the working population from Sierra and surrounding counties. The rest of the businesses in town got what was left. No other local employer could match the wage and benefit packages of the two largest companies, but every worker wanted to get as close as possible, and a 35% gap was unacceptable. In addition, the Kane work force had returned to work for exactly the same money as the original offer five months earlier. I had to find a way to get more money to them, but I knew that we would have to produce meaningful and measurable results to get top management to stay with us.

Every measurement of success in manufacturing was in the toilet. Measurements of profit (there was none), quality, productivity, and on-time delivery were off-the-chart low. The only thing that was high was the amount of scrap produced. Needless to say, morale among both labor and management was about as low as it could be. One indicator of that was the United Way campaign that ran in October after work resumed in August. That was the only fund-raising effort that was allowed in the plant each year, and Kane had always been pretty successful in soliciting employee contributions. The union employees usually generated several thousand dollars in pledges annually. *Not one of them donated!* This was a great example of their solidarity in boycotting any management driven program.

On my trip to Houston, I became enamored of gain-sharing. The seminar hosts contended that this vehicle created a win-win situation between the company and the employees. It was based on improvements in productivity—the amount of goods produced in a given number of direct labor hours. The presenter assured the participants that, with improvements in productivity, all of the other metrics, including profit, would rise proportionally. The company would then split the value of those productivity improvements 50-50 with the work force. Every production employee, direct or indirect, would get an equal per-hour share regardless of his job.

## A QUICK LOOK AT HOW THE WIN-WIN GAIN-SHARING PLAN WORKED

- Let's say the average wage was $8 an hour, and historically 10 units of work were produced in each direct labor hour.
- The labor cost of each unit of work was eighty cents ($8 divided by 10).
- With the plan in effect, if we produce 12 units of work per direct labor hour, the cost decreases to 66.7 cents per unit ($8 divided by 12).
- Let's say we have 100 direct and 50 indirect employees. In a four-week period, they work a total of 24,000 hours (40 x 4 x 150). 16,000 (40 x 4 x100) of those hours were direct labor (the basis of our calculation).
- Previously, those 16,000 direct labor hours would have produced 160,000 units of work (16,000 x 10). Now, given the increased productivity, the same amount of direct labor produces 192,000 units of work (16,000 x 12).

- Before Win-Win, it would have cost $153,000 (192,000 x .80) to produce 192,000 units of work. Now it costs $128,064 (192,000 x .667)—a savings of $24,936.
- When that money is split 50-50, the company keeps $12,468 (24,936 x .5), and the hourly work force has the same amount to divide among them, based on the total hours each worked in the four-week period.
- If we apply that savings to the total hours of the entire work force, each hour on the clock is worth 52 cents (12,468 divided by 24,000). This example would produce a Win-Win bonus check of $83.20 (.52 x 40 x4). Every four-week period stands on its own and is measured against the pre-plan baseline.

Many of my fellow students at the seminar asked questions in the nature of changing the 50-50 to 60-40 in favor of the company or even 75-25. The presenters stood firm in their position that to mess with the split makes management look cheap and insincere, and trust will be lost. They also predicted, correctly, that the direct workers would argue that they should get more than the indirect ones since they actually produced the work to be measured. The class was advised that that is not negotiable because the direct workers could not do their jobs if the set-up men, quality control specialists, and other necessary indirect workers didn't perform. Management was actually put in the position of encouraging solidarity among the union members in allowing their indirect brothers to be included equally. I realized that the beauty of the program was in its simplicity—50-50, the same for all, and only a few numbers in the formula. Those were all factors that can facilitate trust.

The seminar hosts had said that gain-sharing created a win-win situation between the company and the employees. It was 1979, and I had never heard the term win-win. I thought how descriptive it was. So I named the program the Win-Win Gain-sharing Plan and headed back to Philadelphia to present my idea to Robert E.

Robert E scheduled for me to meet with his entire operations committee, which included the eleven vice-presidents that reported to him. The most vocal was the vice-president of personnel, Ed O'Shaughnessy. (I don't think the term human relations had become popular yet.) He was a tall red-haired Irishman with a ruddy complexion indicative of one who drank to excess. He was known as Red Ed to his close associates to differentiate him from another Ed on the operations committee. I had hardly begun to present the wonders of my discovery when Ed jumped to his feet knocking his chair over behind him and started yelling almost as if I had told him he was going to screw his wife. It came to light later that I would not have been the first within the company to do that, but I digress. As his face turned fire-engine red, Ed protested, "This is nothing but a Goddamn incentive plan, and you all know that Kane has an absolute policy against incentive plans. Robert E, I can't believe you even let this guy into the room. Let's move on to the next agenda item."

I realized that the difference between a gain-sharing plan and an incentive plan was too subtle to be explained in the heat of the moment. Plus, I didn't think I could have even convinced myself of the difference. This was no time to back off. I decided to go on the offensive. I looked directly at Robert E without speaking. I hoped that Robert E would be as intimidated by my silent stare as I had been in his office a few weeks earlier. Of course, I also knew that this man had not been intimidated since his big brother kicked him in the nuts when he was three.

Robert E tolerated my stare for a few seconds, and then I spoke. "Robert E, this is my machete." He replied in as respectful a tone as men of his ilk can muster, "OK, Joe. You go back to Indiana and put your plan in place, but it better work—and it better work soon." I was thrilled to learn that Robert E knew my name. I glanced at Red Ed whose face was still bright red and who appeared just to want the meeting to end so that he could get to the bottle of Wild Turkey hidden in his desk. I left with a smug sense of victory even though I had a huge selling job ahead of me with the union and with my own plant management team. At least, I reckoned that I had a chance.

The union had elected a new president, Sam Neff, at the end of the strike. He was a machine operator who had been instrumental in bringing the union back to work. He and I had a positive relationship and were mutually committed to the well-being of both sides of the labor-management structure. Sam encouraged the union rank and file to support the plan, telling them they had nothing to lose. Sam also sold the idea of a common bonus amount for all.

In the first month of the plan, productivity increased slightly, and the work force earned an 11 cent an hour bonus. This was paid in a single check a week after the end of the four-week period. An employee who had worked the normal 160 hours received a check for $17.60 less taxes—not a fortune, but it was noticed. As we were advised in Houston, we issued the bonus on special checks clearly marked Win-Win Bonus and distributed them on a different day than our regular payday. I always suspected that many wives were never aware of these checks, but that was none of my business.

By the end of the third month, the plant was seeing measurably less scrap and more on-time deliveries. The bonus was up to 42 cents an hour or a monthly gross of $67.20. The plant even turned a small profit for the quarter. A year passed, and scrap and rework had decreased remarkably. Orders were shipped 95% on time. As a result, demand was increasing because credibility with customers had been restored. In the first full year of Win-Win, profit exceeded our annual plan by 30%. Win-Win checks had consistently reached triple digits. The plant was back from the depths. My first **MACHETE MOMENT.**

Even then, the plan had its detractors in top management. Ed O'Shaughnessy continued to insist that profit could have increased twice as much if the company had not given half of it away. I'm sure there were other factors that contributed to the improvement, but I'm also sure that it would not have happened without Win-Win. Red Ed could go to hell. He just didn't get it.

By the way, there's at least one Ed O'Shaughnessy in every organization. He's the guy who is against everything that he does not create. He may disguise his negativity as devil's advocacy and imply that he is being constructive. BULLSHIT! Devil's advocates are the worst kind of destructive force when it comes to innovation because they don't have the balls to say they're against an idea. They try to subtly get the rest of the team to decide for themselves that an idea is bad. Weed devil's advocates out of your organization. They are a cancer on your team.

Sam and I formed an unofficial partnership dedicated to the success of the plant and its people. The partnership worked amazingly well for eight years. In the twelve months before the strike, the 400 member union had filed 457 grievances. In the year after they returned, under Sam's leadership, there were four. He did a great job of representing the perspective of the hourly workers, and I believe I did a pretty good job of listening and responding to their needs while remaining true to the best interests of the company.

In addition to the implementation of Win-Win, some little things were done that cost almost nothing. Each made a small difference, and together they were significant. A few weeks after the first Win-Win bonus was paid, I asked the maintenance supervisor to bring two of his men to the factory entrance. I instructed them to dismantle the time clocks and throw them away in the sight of as many union members as possible. The employees and, even more, the management/supervision team were shocked. They had trouble accepting my expectation that we were going to trust our union employees to write down their hours. That had been the procedure with the non-union office people for many years, and there had been no problems. Why would this be different?

I always thought there was something inherently wrong and demeaning about having to wait on line at a clock to go to work or to go to lunch or to go home. Of course, in the twenty-first century, the time clock is a distant memory most places having been replaced by a chip in a badge, but in 1979 this was a revolutionary action.

The custom at the plant had been that the nine prime parking places were marked reserved by name for the plant manager and his management staff. The next day after the time clock action, I rounded up our maintenance guys again and led them to the parking lot. I asked them to take down every one of the reserved signs.

The first-shift hourly employees started work each day at 6:30. Management usually came in at 8. I got to work early the next day to watch the reaction unfold. Even though the signs were gone, no one parked in the previously reserved spaces at 6:30. Then, as 8 AM approached, one after another, the management people took their previously assigned spaces as if they were as entitled as the Queen of England. Sam and I spent that day going to every employee to explain the new way of life. As I anticipated, our words were met with glee by union workers. I also correctly predicted that the reaction from managers would not be so accepting. All except two of the managers yelped in protest. They did not at all appreciate my position that we were all employees of the same company and, thereby, were on the same team and had equal rights. Management employees made more money, and they should have been satisfied with that. However, when it came down to basic rights, everyone was equal. In the future, whenever the managers arrived, they (and I) could take the best available space, and if that meant walking in the rain, so be it. If they wanted their former space, they should come to work at 6:25.

Within a few months, we had ripped out the time clocks and reserved parking signs and had put our money where our mouths were on the issue of productivity. Some would call those grandstand plays, and I would not necessarily disagree. In a really critical situation with people, it often takes revolutionary actions to get their attention and to jump start change. You don't have time for evolutionary changes to take effect. Caution and patience are reserved for the time when you have already gained some credibility. Remember the first priority that I determined on the way home from my first meeting with Robert E—gaining the trust of the work force. Those three actions put us well on the way to accomplishing that goal. Three **MACHETE MOMENTS.**

# After Survival Mode

At the end of the labor contract three years later, the negotiation included the abolishment of the Win-Win plan. The point had been reached where trust between labor and management had grown to allow the plant to operate in a more conventional manner. We had also overhauled the plant with technology improvements so that conditions had changed significantly. The original baseline was no longer meaningful. At that point, the company folded in the average of Win-Win bonuses in the final year of the contract and granted a fair across the board increase on top of that. The Win-Win plan was no more. It had served its purpose. The offer was accepted with an 80% approval.

As time went by, and the plant established a momentum of profitability, management made other small gestures to embrace the work force. Just before Christmas 1982, I bought two ping pong tables and a Foosball game and had them delivered to the break room on a Sunday. I wrapped a ribbon around them and put a large sign on them. It read, "Merry Christmas to our favorite people. Have some fun on your breaks. Just don't fight." Beginning the next Monday, and throughout the remainder of my administration, the toys were well used and not abused.

Given the large rural population in our region, pitching horse shoes was a popular recreational activity. Pre-dating my tenure, three pits outside the factory were kept busy over lunch time and breaks. A couple of the regular pitchers showed up at my office one day with a request. Could they clear out an unused corner of the factory and install indoor horse shoe pits? They would install them at their expense and would put a safety fence around them so that no one could get hit by a bouncing shoe. And they would not infringe on their time on the clock. I had no reason to say no, so I said okay. Those pits are still in use today and, as far as anyone at Kane knows, they are the only indoor horse shoe pits anywhere.

These were minute gestures that cost little, but done consistently over time, they made a huge statement. They said that management cared about making the employees' experience at work as pleasant as possible. And more than that, they said that the people were trusted not to abuse the privileges. Some employees may have done other things I didn't like, but I was never aware of anyone who took advantage of these considerations. Although there were still some sore-asses among both management/ supervision employees and union members, the message of trust carried over to the vast majority.

I went into this job with virtually no specific qualifications to manage a manufacturing operation. Come to think of it, that didn't change much in the thirty-four years I held management positions. All I had was an ability to visualize what could and should be and to organize and manage people. Then I had the good sense to get the hell out of their way, and let them do their jobs. All the while, I was there to show them the goal line and support them in supplying the necessary tools and education. I considered it my responsibility to ensure that they consistently worked as a team and to buffer them from harm from both inside and outside the organization.

I did have one ace in the hole—I retained just enough of my accounting background to distinguish between valid numbers and bullshit. Over the years, I have played that ace many times with my own colleagues, suppliers, and customers. It is a great asset.

There were a few casualties as a result of our new way of doing business.

I inherited a plant superintendent, a production manager, a personnel manager, and a cadre of foremen who were all old school. Most of the job titles from the early-eighties have been replaced by new-age titles such as team leader and human relations manager, but the jobs are essentially the same.

The plant superintendent, Frank Mayerling, had been a machine operator at Kane's Akron, Ohio plant for fifteen years. He had moved to Vienna when the plant relocated eighteen years earlier. Part of his decision to move was based on the promise of being promoted to foreman. Shortly before the big strike, Frank had been promoted to plant superintendent, a position on the plant manager's management staff. At that time, all jobs at that level had required the wearing of a tie to work every day. He had a black clip-on that he wore proudly with a heavily starched white shirt as his badge of success. Poor guy; he had waited 33 years for the right to wear a tie to work, and now he was working for this inexperienced plant manager who wore sport shirts and jeans. He asked me one day if it would be okay if he continued to wear his white shirt and tie. I told him of course it would. There was no dress code except the requirement to be clean. He still didn't understand, but that answer seemed to allow him to find peace.

Frank's running mate, in the role of production manager, was Jerry Keyes, who had been hired as an expediter (another obsolete position) at the time of the plant startup in 1961. He too had been promoted through the ranks to his Peter Principle level. For those youngsters out there who are not familiar with this reference, *The Peter Principle* was developed by Dr. Laurence Peter in his 1968 book of the same title.

Dr. Peter states that in an organizational hierarchy, eventually almost every employee will rise to his level of incompetence. The Peter Principle is based on the notion that employees will get promoted as long as they are competent, but at some point, they will land in a job that is too challenging for them. Employees rise to their level of incompetence and stay there. Over time, every position in the hierarchy will be filled by someone who is not competent to carry out his new duties. Dr. Peter sums up the Peter Principle by saying, "The cream rises until it sours."

Remember, Dr. Peter's book was written in the sixties when, if you were with a company for three years, you pretty much had a job for life. Companies ended up overstaffed because a large number of their employees had become deadwood. That phenomenon has all but disappeared now that periodic downsizing has become a way of life in order for companies to stay competitive.

Frank and Jerry, whose jobs called for them to be in sync with each other's every move, despised each other. Time after time, I would get a story of a problem from one, and hear an entirely different version when I checked with the other. I finally told them that neither of them was allowed to come to me unless he brought the other. I hoped they would get the message that my faith in them was wearing thin. I never actually found out. In less than a year, Frank died within weeks after being diagnosed with cancer. Jerry lasted a couple of years before I finally bit the bullet and helped him to an early retirement. I thought I had been pretty fair to Jerry. He was 58, and I saw to it that he received full retirement benefits and gave him the traditional retirement party where his co-workers could come and say nice things about him.

The personnel manager was a different case. He was a third generation Kane employee who had ascended to a considerably higher position at the plant than his grandfather, father, uncle, and brother had achieved. He was Don (for Donatello) Ferrari. While the family was Italian through and through and spoke as if every comment was a veiled threat, Don was the milquetoast member of the family. He tried to talk tough, but there was nothing in him that suggested he could back up his talk. Actually, he was a bit of a laughingstock among the work force—both management and labor. That's truly not a good image for your HR manager.

My strongest memory of Don came immediately before the strike. The vote on the offer was on a Saturday morning. My predecessor as plant manager had called a meeting of all exempt employees in the plant conference room to await the result. Don was there with a bucket of white paint and a wide brush. He delivered an evil sounding laugh as he declared to all of us, "If those bastards go out, I'm going to paint a white line across the driveway. If any of those assholes on the picket line step across it, I'm calling the cops.' The dumb son-of-a-bitch actually went out and painted the line minutes after the word of the strike vote reached us. The only visible result of that action was that it gave the picketers a target to cover with roofing nails for the tires of anyone who dared to drive in or out. I think the only one who benefitted from the strike was the owner of the tire store where we sent our office employees to have their tires repaired or replaced at company expense.

After the strike, Don lasted only a few weeks. We were going to establish a new way of doing things, and there was no possibility that he would ever understand. I had to get someone in that position who would be respected, and Don clearly was not that person. I actually hired a woman, Jo Ann Bailey into the job—another unheard of action that shook up the troops. She did an outstanding job of working with the union and in all the other facets of her position. Jo Ann was a major factor in the success the plant was to enjoy throughout the next decade.

Attrition took a few of the others on the management and supervision team that I had inherited, and before long there was a cohesive group that bought into our new philosophy of trust and respect. Almost before I knew it, I had been in the job for seven profitable years with little conflict. Management and the union had negotiated two new contracts without work stoppages.

# The Beginning of the End

In December 1986, it was time for the bi-annual election for union president. Sam Harden had run unopposed in all elections since the strike, but this year was different. At the last minute, Harry Gutman filed to run. Harry had been union president during the last three strikes including the long, violent one of 1978. As you would suspect from that track record, he was absolutely anti-company and unreasonable in any attempt to compromise. Remember the 457 pre-strike grievances? He ran on a one plank platform: Sam and I had gotten too close, and Sam no longer objectively represented the best interests of the workers. It didn't matter that jobs were more secure than ever before, or that corporate management had just committed to investing in an expansion of the plant.

Mr. Gutman rounded up enough dissidents to support him, and they ran roughshod over those who just wanted to come to work every day and do their jobs. Against all reason, Harry Gutman was elected to a two-year term as union president, and the next day I put my resume on the street. To this day, I can't comprehend what would drive anyone to vote for that asshole.

This makes for an interesting story about how years can change one's perspective. In the eighteen years after the plant moved from Akron, there had been six work stoppages at the end of labor contracts each of which was three years in duration. Do the math. Every time a new contract was presented, it was rejected by the union. *Six times in a row!* Of course, management said that the union was impossible to work with. And the union said the company was unfair. As I look back from a third of a century later, I realize we were both right to some degree.

Using that same hindsight, it might have been true that the leadership provided by Sam and me had grown stale. I don't think we had done anything particularly wrong. We were just worn out in our jobs and in our partnership. A few years later, I admitted that I had had nothing new to bring to the party. Sometimes it takes a hurtful blow to make one realize the obvious. In this case, the obvious was that Joe Camarte's time as manager of this plant had run its course. I worked with a marketing director at Kane, who once told me that I was one of the greatest dragon-slayers he ever knew but that I wasn't that good at catching mice. I think my Kane Power Industries experience indicated that he might have been accurate in his observation.

In the second month of Gutman's new term, there was a blizzard that produced two feet of snow. It had started a little before midnight, and it was still snowing at dawn, so there had been no opportunity to clean any streets. The third-shift supervisors had wisely sent their people home about midnight, based on the forecast and the fact that the snow and wind had already started. About 4 AM, as was the custom in such instances, I notified all of the radio stations in Sierra and surrounding counties that Kane would be closed on first and second shifts. Employees should listen to the radio for reports pertaining to third-shift and beyond. Two union employees, who lived nearby, did not hear the message and made it in to work on first-shift.

Harry Gutman used the fact that those two had gotten to work as the basis for a grievance that claimed that closing the plant constituted a lockout, and all 400 union employees would have to be paid for eight hours. That grievance went to arbitration and was upheld by the arbitrator. Unbelievable! I swore that I would never close a workplace again because of weather, and I never have. My policy at Kane, and in subsequent stops in my career, became that the company would forgive absence in questionable weather. There would be no mark against an employee who didn't come to work, but the operation would always be open for those who were able to make it in.

I have no problem with the concept of unions. They came about because there was a time when management policies relating to pay, hours, and working conditions took advantage of workers. Workers didn't create the union movement—employers did through their greed. I personally think that the middleman isn't necessary if management treats its people with consideration. But it's naïve to expect that of all companies. I contend that if unions were outlawed, within two or three years we would be right back to the 1920's in the relationship between management and employees. I think that the strongest position for today's line worker is not the existence of a union, but the threat of one. No manager is likely to survive a successful union organization on his watch.

I guess Harry won because in April 1988, sixteen months after he was elected, I resigned to accept a better opportunity. A couple of days before I was to leave, I sat in on a grievance hearing in Jo Ann Bailey's office with Harry Gutman and two of his union stewards. Although I had pledged to myself to keep a civil tongue, that became impossible as I watched Gutman pound his fist on Jo Ann's desk and shout his frivolous claim. I told Gutman that he could not have done more damage to the company and its employees, including the ones he was supposed to represent, if he were Satan himself. He said he felt the same about me. I have never seen Harry Gutman again, and I'm sure that's okay with both of us.

When the last contract that was signed during my term expired in 1990, I was long gone. But I watched with great interest as Harry Gutman took his union members out on a strike that lasted six weeks. They returned for ten cents an hour more than the original offer. It would take fifteen years to recover the money each of them lost due to the strike.

# A Life Lesson

I get lessons in life from some unusual places. Throughout my career, I have observed the wisdom of the 1955 film, *The Seven-Year Itch,* which starred Marilyn Monroe and Tom Ewell. The premise was that Ewell's character, after seven years of a rather routine marriage, was tempted to stray to Marilyn's character when his wife took the kids to visit her mother for the summer. This left him in the city with Marilyn living in the next apartment. Even the most faithful of husbands might have had difficulty resisting the charms of Ms. Monroe, but don't tell Kate I said that. The lesson I took from the movie was that anything can become humdrum after seven years and that it would not be unusual to feel the need for a major change. Later, I amended my theory to include a clause that the change can be either a total divorce from your current situation or a radical restructuring of your existing life. This theory fits me to a tee.

I have never experienced the problem in my marriage, which has just completed its forty-eighth very happy year. However, I have seen the itch very clearly in other parts of my life, especially in my career. Of course, seven years on the nose is not magic, but it's a good average of the amount of time it takes until some extreme action is needed. There comes a point when evolutionary change isn't enough.

In my case, I spent six years in the sixties drifting through four different jobs before realizing I needed to settle down and find something for the long haul. Once at Kane, I was in the accounting department for seven years before getting myself transferred to manufacturing operations. I was plant manager for eight years, but most of the final year I was committed to leaving and was looking for a place to land.

# I'm Outta' Here

Going away parties are often held when a long-term employee leaves a job either by retirement, transfer, or just moving on. My friends and co-workers at Kane threw such an event for me at a local hotel. It was a nice affair, fairly routine as those things go, with a cocktail hour followed by dinner and the presentation of some gifts and kind words. About seventy people from the office and supervision ranks and even a few union members were there. Several brought their spouses, so there were about a hundred people in all. It was an opportunity for them and me to wish each other good fortune and to say how much we had enjoyed working together. In about 90% of the cases, I was sincere, and I believe they were too.

Near the end of the meal, I noticed Jerry Keyes and his wife come in quietly. They sat alone at a small table off to the side of the group. You remember Jerry. He's the one whom I had treated fairly (my perspective) in expediting his retirement a few years earlier. They didn't eat and rejected the server's offer to bring them a drink.

After dessert, Jo Ann Bailey got up and tapped on her glass to gain the attention of the group. She made about five minutes of comments, mostly complimentary, some humorous, some jokingly insulting, but all well-meant. Then she presented me with some gifts on behalf of the company and the employees. Next, she asked me to say a few words. I had not prepared a formal speech, but I spent about five minutes recalling some good times and thanking people. The next step at these affairs is always to invite comments from the audience. About a half-dozen of my friends came to the podium to tell funny or poignant anecdotes about my career. It was all very heart-warming.

Then, when it appeared to be all but over, here came Jerry Keyes to the microphone. I swear this is a quote I will never forget. He said, "I started at Kane Power right after it opened in 1961. At that time, I worked for Tom McKittrick (since deceased), and I thought he was the biggest prick I could ever work for. But I was wrong. Joe Camarte is the biggest prick I ever met." And he sat down never to be seen by me again. When the after-party milling around started, Jerry and his wife had left the building. I have never been angry about that moment. In fact, I have not even disagreed with Jerry's disclosure when I've looked at it from his perspective.

If you are ever honored by (subjected to) one of these events, here is my advice. Accept that the organizers and most in attendance like and/or respect you and intend for you to feel good about what will happen there. There will be some, however, who don't like you and will take this opportunity to let you know what they think. These people are much akin to the devil's advocates I discussed earlier. They will mask their comments in a costume of humor, but they won't be funny. Enjoy the good part of your party, and let the assholes appear to go unnoticed by you.

## III.

# A HODGE-PODGE OF SERIOUS THOUGHTS, THINGS THAT PISS ME OFF, AND SILLINESS

## Philosophy

Early in my management career, I thought it was advisable to list the values by which I was going to be guided throughout my professional and personal life. I have amended the list a little over the years, but it is still pretty much as I originally wrote it. There are ten tenets.

1.  THE GOLDEN RULE. I am in no way a religious person. However, I believe this is the most valuable guideline for anyone. If everyone lived to the letter of this rule, the only laws we would need would be housekeeping items such as "Drive on the right side of the street." There would be no murder or theft or lying or screwing each other's spouses.
2.  LOYALTY. I am fiercely loyal to those people I care about and/ or to whom I have made a commitment. I will never knowingly betray them in any way and will support their every endeavor to the best of our ability.
3.  TRUST. My take on this is possibly a bit counter-intuitive. When I meet a new person, my default position is to trust her. I believe most people are wary until the new acquaintance earns their trust.

Do I ever get burned by taking this position? You bet! On those occasions where my trust has proven to have been misplaced as shown by a deliberate act of betrayal, the guilty party is scratched from my trusted list, and it is very difficult for her ever to return. However, most of the time, the relationship develops faster and becomes stronger than it would have by waiting for trust to be earned.

4. AVOID TOO MUCH POLICING. Too much time, money, and energy are spent in protecting things that are not worth protecting. We stand on nickels while hundred dollar bills blow out the window. "Let's put a $10,000 security system in the vending machine area so that no one can break in and steal a candy bar." Bullshit! Employ some common sense for decisions that pertain to policing.

5. BUILD MUTUAL RESPECT IN RELATIONSHIPS WITH OTHERS. While I believe trust can be given, I think respect develops over time based on shared experiences and observed actions. It starts with being considerate of the feelings and needs of others and grows through a combination of continued consideration, honesty, intelligent decisions, hard work, and a variety of other factors.

6. A BIAS TO SAY YES. When an employee or an acquaintance asks me for something over which I have control, and I don't have a specific reason to say no, I say yes. Why wouldn't I? I see many authority figures put people through the wringer just because they can. Apparently, they like to show their superiority of position. An employee might ask me, "Can I have tomorrow off?" If saying yes doesn't put me or my colleagues in an untenable situation, the answer is yes. She might want to tell me why as a courtesy, but I really don't have to know. The only important facts are that she wants off and that granting the request will not cause undue hardship to me or others.

7. INTELLECTUAL HONESTY. Everyone should have honesty as part of his philosophy, but this is an extension of basic honesty. Intellectual honesty is the answering of a question that the other person did not ask. However, it is a vital extension of the question

he *did* ask. A customer calls to say, "I will be flying my small private single engine plane to your town today, and I want to know how the weather is?" I reply, "Oh, it's beautiful—sunny, 75, no wind." That's honest as far as it goes, but there should be more. What I didn't say was, "You'd better plan to get here before 4 o'clock because severe thunderstorms with high winds are in the forecast for late afternoon." That is intellectually honest. Yes and no answers are fine for the witness stand, but when you know what a person is looking for, it is intellectually dishonest not to give it to him just because he didn't ask all the right questions.

8.  EMBRACE THOSE WHO LOVE AND RESPECT YOU AND WHOM YOU LOVE AND RESPECT, AND RID YOURSELF OF THOSE WHO WILL ONLY BRING YOU DOWN. No explanation is necessary.

9.  KNOW YOUR PRIORITIES. Many years ago, I identified my priorities: family, job, friends, and community. Everything else falls in line behind those. I only pay attention to other matters when there is no demand from the top four.

    My parents grew up in the depression era. Standards were extremely different back then. They used to tell me that clothes make the man. How shallow I think that is. As important as that was to them, it could never have been a priority of mine. I think it has been a reaction to that belief that I have not made it a priority to be fashionable in my choice of clothing. I have extended that to an opinion that is not necessary to gather material things. However, I do wish I had my baseball cards back that my mother got rid of when I went to college in 1958. There was a Mickey Mantle rookie card among them.

10. QUESTION AUTHORITY. We are all fallible. Just because someone outranks you, is no reason to assume she is always right. Whether it comes from an individual or a company or a government, we should not accept an idea that, after a reasonable amount of investigation, we believe is wrong. I'm not recommending that you become a scofflaw, but if your disagreement with a law or a rule or a decision is serious enough, you should give it your best effort to get it changed. Actually, I don't consider civil disobedience

out of the question, but you had better understand the possible consequences before you act. Following simple logic, the other side of this coin is that we should listen and give consideration to those who question us when we are the authority.

I hold myself to these principles. When I slip, it is never deliberate, and I correct the error as soon as possible. I also require others in management or supervisory positions in my jurisdiction to abide by them. Compliance is a condition of ongoing employment, and disregard of these principles cannot be balanced by any amount of positive characteristics.

## Can We Mine Deeper When It Comes to Contributing Ideas?

For years, I have pondered the value of quantifying brainpower. As a result, I have developed a theory that you are welcome to use as your own where you work.

It's an art for a leader to be able to encourage disagreement without spending an inordinate amount of time listening to whiners. I'm not saying that you should create a democracy in running a business. Consensus is overrated. It's nice to reach it, but as the boss, the big decisions are yours to make. However, listening to, and even soliciting, the opinions presented by others can be extremely valuable and should often be part of the process leading to a decision.

In that vein, I would like to expose you to the Camarte Theory of Collective Brainpower, which is based on absolutely no empirical data. The basis is fifty years of observation as an adult. Brainpower for the purpose of this piece is a combination of intelligence, wisdom, education, experience, common sense, and intuition. I don't have a formula for the proportion of each makes up the whole. It really doesn't matter.

We all know what an organization chart looks like. The boss is at the top, and there are levels of employees below her, each reporting to someone on the level above and always making less money than those at higher levels. Let's pretend our company has four levels and that each level has three times as many people as the level immediately above. For purposes of this exercise, everyone at a given level possesses twice the Brainpower (BP) as those at the next level down. Our chart would look like this:

## CAMARTE THEORY OF COLLECTIVE BRAINPOWER

| | |
|---|---|
| X | (8 units BP; total 8 units) |
| XXX | (4 units BP each; total 12 units) |
| XXX XXX XXX | (2 units BP each; total 18 units) |
| XXX XXX XXX XXX XXX XXX XXX XXX XXX | (1 unit BP each; total 27 units) |

### TOTAL UNITS OF BRAINPOWER—65

In this example, there are 65 units of Brainpower in the company. The boss has only 12% of the total. He and his direct reports combined have only 31%. Not to find a way to take advantage of the Collective Brainpower of everyone in the organization is downright foolish.

If your ego won't let you accept that you and your managers are only twice as smart as the people on the next level below, use the presumption that each level has four times the Brainpower of the next level down. (That makes the head guy sixteen times as smart as the workers on the factory floor or the case workers or the clerical staff—a premise I have a lot of trouble with.) Even then, the boss has only 23% of the total BP, and he and his lieutenants together have 41%. The truth is that it doesn't matter what reasonable ratio you decide on among the top, the middle, and the bottom of the organization, the majority of the Brainpower is still down in the ranks. I can't imagine how anyone would expect her employees to check their brains at the front door.

A bi-product of this approach is that the people in lesser positions feel more a part of the company. For an employee to feel valued leads to all kinds of positive results.

# Words and Beliefs That I Just Don't Understand

I would never want to insult anyone because of the terminology I use. However, in America, we have diluted the English language, in the name of political correctness, to such an extent that often I don't know what the speaker is talking about. Many of the changes are totally artificial. I think the primary reasons to change a traditionally understood term would be to avoid hurt feelings or to be more accurate. Many of the changes we have had thrust upon our population do neither. Here are a few examples of changes to which I see no point.

- Drink to hydrate
- Secretary to administrative assistant
- Husband/wife to spouse
- Angry to upset
- Arguing to being defensive
- Die to pass
- Religious to faith-based

The ones I've mentioned so far are pretty harmless, driven by pretentiousness or by the much overpopulated advertising world. Other than to be irritating, they don't affect my life one way or another. Although relatively benign, they provide the slippery slope from which the language is diluted where it matters.

Here are some changes that do make a difference because I face them in day-to-day life.

- Mexican to Hispanic (This is a term that was invented by the U.S. government for the 1980 census. It is a convenient term that Americans created to make it easier to complete forms. There is not total agreement among those to whom we apply this label as to whether Hispanic or Latino is better. Or would they rather be attached to their country of origin? There is nothing wrong with referring to a person as a Mexican or a Cuban. If I am in another country, I prefer to be called an American—not a Caucasian from the Western Hemisphere.)
- Poor to socially marginalized or vulnerable
- Mentally ill to emotionally or intellectually impaired

And then there are some that have gone through so many changes that you need a scorecard so that you use the right term. These are examples of political correctness gone berserk.

- Retarded to slow to intellectually challenged (I agree that we needed to find an alternative to the word *retarded* because it has been misused so frequently as an insult. What I don't understand is that the national advocacy organization, which used to be called the Association of Retarded Citizens, is now called ARC. If they want to do away with the term, how can it still be part of their acronym?)

- Shell shock (WWII) to battle fatigue (Korea) to operational exhaustion (Viet Nam) to post-traumatic stress disorder (today)
- Illegal aliens to undocumented to unauthorized (I was in a meeting with 30 people the first time I heard that last term. Not one of us knew the meaning. Everyone wondered "authorized to do what?")
- Slum to ghetto to inner city
- Crippled to handicapped to disabled to physically challenged (I agree that crippled is iffy, but I see nothing wrong with handicapped or disabled.)

There is a tremendous amount of work to be done in human services and education—more than we can complete if we work 24 hours a day for life. Time spent in making irrelevant changes to terminology is wasted and absurd. We should simplify our speech and writing so that it can be understood by those who don't work with the subject in their day-to-day lives. Does anyone actually believe that a poor person feels any better being called socially marginalized or vulnerable? She's poor—not stupid. All of the original terms on the list bring a clear picture immediately to mind. That is what good words do; they have impact. The reason we have words is to communicate a clear picture of the subject, thought, or action. Why do we want to dilute any emotional or logical impact by making up words that don't describe the subject in a simple way that is understandable to all? The new words bring absolutely no emotional reaction to me and do not stir me to action.

While I'm ranting over the use of our language, when did the polite people start calling everything they disagree with *inappropriate*? If you disagree with someone's comment, have the balls to own your disagreement. Then you and the speaker can fight about it. To say that someone is inappropriate disarms the speaker. You have made a unilateral judgment to which there is no reply. Appropriate and inappropriate don't mean the same to everyone and have different connotations depending on the crowd and setting. I've been in places with people who had no objection to my saying to someone, "What the fuck are you talking about?" This is most likely to happen when they are prattling on with no real point to make and with no end of the prattling in sight. In fact, it happens on a fairly regular basis. On the other hand, even I would not stand up in a town meeting and say that. (Usually not—there could be exceptions.) If you grew up in a church atmosphere, different things are inappropriate to you than if you grew up in a locker room environment. I will close on this subject with the summary comment that it is *inappropriate* for us to judge one another as *inappropriate* just because we disagree.

Another annoyance comes from the use of pronouns. I appreciate that women can and should be offended if we always assume the male position—"If someone does something, *he* is whatever." In its typically flawed wisdom, our society has solved this problem by giving us two choices—wrong and cumbersome. It is now quite common to say, "If someone does something, *they* are whatever. There is no *they*; we are talking about one person. *They* calls for multiple people. As I learned in Miss Neptune's eighth grade English class, this is incorrect grammar. As an alternative, we can say *he-or-she* every time our statement calls for a pronoun. It's a pain in the ass to remember to do that. If the statement is referring specifically to a man or a woman, I use the gender specific version. If not, I randomly, but equally, rotate *she, he, her,* and *him*. You will see that practice on display in this book. I hope that isn't confusing. I'm just trying to do the right (or less wrong) thing.

Not all of my displeasure regarding gender comes from misuse of the English language. I believe that other than being on average bigger, stronger, fleeter of foot, and having the ability to easily pee in the forest, men have no innate advantages over women. Through another of my totally unscientific observations, I conclude that women are at least equal to men when it comes to intelligence, emotional stability, leadership ability, honesty, and whatever other characteristics you want to look at. I think it's unconscionable that they have to settle for lesser pay for the same job. I believe that is changing, but progress is far too slow.

The truth is that I cuss. I cuss a lot. In order of frequency per sentence, I cuss during athletic competition, in bars, in day-to-day conversations, at social functions, and in meetings. I don't attend church, but if I did, I would probably have few inhibitions there.

One of my tributes to gender equality is that I talk the same around women as I do with men. I cringe when I hear a man say, "I can't say what I think because there are ladies present." Or if he slips and says damn, he apologizes to any women who may have heard him.

I'm sure that I offend some women *and* some men with my language, and that is unfortunate. If you take the position that all swearing is out of order, especially if you don't know that it is acceptable to the people you are with, I won't totally disagree with you. Even I try to watch it in groups of strangers or those that I know will be offended. But I also don't think that use of those words is unpardonable. They are just words and, as such, are totally harmless. On the other hand, the use of "polite words" to spread misinformation, prejudice, or things that are just plain none of your fucking business can be extremely harmful. So who's the bad guy? The one who uses mother-fucker with humorous intent? Or the guy who says he has nothing against black people as long as they stay in their place? Or the woman who whispers to her bridge club that the fifteen-year old neighbor girl is pregnant? I'll take the mother-fucker every time.

"You always know where Joe stands and what he thinks." Throughout my career in both the manufacturing and non-profit worlds, I have heard this observation hundreds of times. I agree with it and am proud to own it. However, I believe that, more often than not, it is meant, at least partially, in a derogatory way. Why should this characteristic be so uncommon that it would even be commented upon? Just last week I heard a colleague say, "I wish I could be as forthright as Joe." Why should this be a wish? Just do it.

Our society has developed such paranoia about being considered politically incorrect that we don't say what we mean anymore. The do-gooders have even rewritten history to match what they wish were true. To make matters worse, the rewrite has been accepted as truth by much of our population. Most of our founding fathers including Benjamin Franklin, Thomas Paine, Thomas Jefferson, and George Washington were not Christians. They were Deists. They thought the universe had a creator, but that the creator does not directly communicate with humans, either by revelation or by 2000 year old books. Deists do not accept the inconsistencies of superstitions and unsubstantiated stories that are so prevalent in Christianity, Judaism, and all of the other popular religions. They believe in reason over myth.

Nowhere does the Constitution say: "The United States is a Christian nation", or anything even close to that. In fact, the words *Jesus Christ, Christianity, Bible, Creator, and God* are never mentioned in the Constitution. Nowhere in the Constitution is religion mentioned, except to exclude it from the processes of government. There were some pretty smart fellows before and after our nation's founding who shared that belief. That list includes Aristotle and Plato, Albert Einstein and Stephen Hawking, Abraham Lincoln, and Neil Armstrong.

It really disgusts me when some jock falls to his knees in prayer when he scores a touchdown. Does he actually think God cares who wins the Super Bowl but doesn't give a damn about stopping genocide in Rwanda, or the guy next door kicking the piss out of his wife and kids every night? How do you suppose he feels about people who dehumanize those of races, genders, life-styles, and others who aren't just like them?

# Silliness

I'm reminded of an exercise some friends and I went through recently at our after-tennis beer drinking session. The core of this group has played tennis together about three times a week for forty years. And for forty years on Wednesday evenings, we have gone out for a couple of beers afterwards. (Actually, it used to be more than a couple, but age and punishments for getting caught have changed our lifestyles. That woman who founded MADD should get more credit than she does for driving a significant change for the better throughout our entire society.) We discuss many topics, some deep and some absurd. Sometimes our conversations are spontaneous; sometimes one of the guys puts forth an agenda topic by email before the gathering. More and more, we travel down memory lane, but I think that is caused by a combination of not creating many new memories and our faltering short-term memories.

Speaking of short-term versus long-term memory, here's my favorite personal example. My Dad took me to my first big league ball game in Cleveland in 1948. I can remember the entire starting lineup of the Indians that day, but I can't tell you what I had for breakfast this morning. For the Tribe, there were Jim Hegan, Eddie Robinson, Joe Gordon, Lou Boudreau (who was also the manager), Ken Keltner, Dale Mitchell, Larry Doby, Bob Kennedy, and Bob Lemon was on the mound. Satchel Paige relieved in the eighth inning. Keltner sprained his ankle in the fourth inning and was replaced by utility infielder, Johnny Beradino, who later spent thirty-six years as Dr. Steve Hardy, the star of the daytime soap opera, *General Hospital.*

On the evening I'm talking about, I suggested an agenda item that had been on my mind for some time. I wanted the group to define and differentiate among derogatory terms we apply to those we don't like or respect. As the discussion evolved, four terms bubbled to the top—*prick, dick, jerk*, and *asshole*. It was important to define those terms so that, at least among ourselves, we could be clear about our opinion of someone. Here are the results of that study.

You paid for the book, so you have permission to use them as your own. We have deliberately not copyrighted our findings, choosing instead to place them in the public domain. If we get the word out among a large enough segment of the population, we can all relate to one another's feelings. Maybe we can even have them translated into multiple languages or make a candid-camera type video showing real-life examples of each. Here you go.

- A *prick* is one who is deliberately mean-spirited toward some individual(s) or group(s). It requires some amount of intelligence and skill to be a prick. We all agreed that we can respect a prick for his ability even though we don't want to associate with him. We can even laugh at his comments and actions as long as his prickishness is not directed at us. A prick is often successful, by his own standards, at one or more facets of his life.
- A *dick* is a watered down version of a prick. In fact, one of the guys vehemently contended that dick is a sub category of prick and does not deserve its own category. At that point, someone ordered another round, and the conversation reverted to reminiscences of matches played in our lost youth. We never actually reached consensus on the dick the issue.

- A *jerk* is usually unintentional in his flaws but seems to do and say the wrong thing much of the time. He is usually not mean-spirited. For the most part, he just doesn't get it.
- An *asshole* is, well, an *asshole*. He has few redeeming virtues and is always capable of saying or doing the wrong thing in a mean-spirited manner. He is generally not as intelligent as a prick.

Finally, in a demonstration of our commitment to equality, we decided that all of the terms can apply to either gender.

# IV.

# MY MANUFACTURING CAREER—PART TWO

## The Inherited Situation

I was hired by Thursby Plastics, Inc. in 1988 to start and manage its new Indiana plant. Thursby was a relatively small manufacturer of heavy duty plastics. Its plant and headquarters were in western North Carolina. The company offered multiple product lines that, in aggregate, yielded annual revenue of about $140 million.

The line that was to be transferred to the Indiana plant was a very profitable product that filled a small niche industrial market of which Thursby had about a 95% share. Annual sales were a little under $40 million. The product was a small single-purpose container utilizing the processes of injection molding and fabricating and was made in several sizes. There were four primary customers that made up about 90% of that business and a handful of other customers.

The North Carolina plant was running at capacity. Management decided that rather than expand its home plant, they would build in Indiana so that the manufacturing of this product would be closer to its customer base in the upper Midwest. The plan was that the North Carolina plant would continue to make all the other products.

The company was privately owned by its founder, Cecil Thursby. His family consisted of his wife, Elvina, and six grown children. Jackie, who was about thirty, was the only other family member involved in the

36

business. He said that he did not want to participate in the management of the company. However, he saw his connection as his insurance policy to keep the company in the family. The other siblings all owned stock in the company.

One problem that I was unaware of on the way in was the fact that the business, including the profitable part was in shambles from a lack of qualified leadership. Cecil was an inherently good man—a brilliant engineer, but he was short on management skills. He had entrusted the management of the company to a small cadre of long-term employees, some of whom were even more inadequate. Those factors created a perfect storm that led to chaos, uncertainty, and red ink.

When I started, a local firm, Lund Construction Company, had just begun work on the new facility. It was June in one of the hottest summers on record. Jack McCloud, Lund's project manager on the job, gave me a construction trailer on site to use as my office. From the trailer, I would be Jack's contact and would hire the startup workforce, including the supervision team. Jack told me that he would try to get me a trailer with air-conditioning as soon as possible. I'm still waiting.

# Cecil and I—Love at First Sight

Cecil was in his mid-sixties when I first met him. He was looking at cities in Indiana in which to locate his new plant. A friend of mine at the local Chamber of Commerce, who knew of my desire to leave Kane Power, was preparing the schedule for his visit. This included looking at potential sites and interviewing some local leaders and candidates for the plant manager job. He booked me as both a community leader and a candidate to manage the operation.

Cecil brought with him Jerry Spade, his vice-president, who had been with the company since its inception. They and my friend from the Chamber toured the community in the morning. In the afternoon, Cecil, Jerry, and I talked for two hours during which I tried to sell them on Vienna and me. Cecil and I were totally enamored of each other. Cecil was quick to disclose his values, and in every case we connected. He talked about commitment to his employees and his community. He was proud of his policy of sharing profits with his employees. He talked about quality and innovation and about the importance of family. Through all that, he seemed humble.

When I got home that evening, I couldn't wait to tell Kate that I had finally met the man I wanted to work for. The next evening, Cecil and Jerry took Kate and me to dinner. Again, Cecil talked on and on. I had heard some of the stories the day before, but I accepted that he was bringing Kate up to speed. I didn't realize that Cecil had a limited repertoire and that I would eventually hear every one of those tales repeated what would seem like a thousand times. On the way home, Kate urged me to be cautious in making my decision, but as always, she supported me in accepting whatever decision I was comfortable with. One thing was certain, I could not have been less satisfied than I had been the last several months at Kane.

A couple of months passed, and a new problem was thrown into the mix. Kane wanted to transfer me to Jonesville, Tennessee. There were several places where Kate and I thought we might be happy living, and Jonesville was nowhere on the list. I was beginning to panic, so I called Cecil. I had learned that he had decided to build in Vienna. I reckoned that he had to be close to making a decision on a plant manager. I explained the exact situation, and really laid it on thickly as to how badly I wanted to come to work for him. I sensed that he was not quite ready to move on that decision, but Cecil at least wanted to introduce me the rest of his management team. He arranged for me to visit North Carolina the next week.

I toured the headquarters and the plant and met the management staff. We all went to dinner together. I was not impressed by most of the managers, but I was in no position to be choosy. I wanted and needed this job. I figured once in the door, I could make something good happen. Little did I know that, within a couple of years, I would be responsible for the fate of the entire organization.

# The Startup

The hiring of the supervisors in Indiana was an interesting process. The plant needed only manufacturing people. All engineering, sales, and administrative functions would remain at headquarters. I would handle all local personnel and accounting requirements. We would start with three shift supervisors and a manufacturing engineer who would also supervise the maintenance staff. Until the plant was up to full strength, the shift supervisors would double with duties in quality assurance, shipping, and other indirect functions. The most qualified non-exempt employees would be asked to be working lead people.

The plan for the startup worked exceedingly well. By the end of July, I had hired four competent men as our supervisors, and we were on our way. Their first assignment was to go to North Carolina for two weeks of training on our product line. Management in North Carolina was impressed with them, and they returned with a good grasp of how the processes worked. The plan was to move machinery in for about 20% of the production until the work became routine for the labor force. The rest would follow over a three-month period so that the entire product line would be in the Indiana plant by the first of the year.

By mid-August, I was ready to hire the production work force. The practice in our area for mass hiring, such as a startup or expansion, was to have a call out of interested candidates at a specified time. The locals called them cattle calls. They were usually held in a large building at the fairgrounds. I always thought it was inconsiderate to make the applicants sit all day until it was their turn to be interviewed. Plus, with multiple interviewers, the candidates were measured by as many different yardsticks as there were interviewers.

I planned to conduct all of the interviews personally by appointment. I ran a three-day ad in the local newspaper and in papers in surrounding towns. Instead of the normal practice, the Thursby want-ad asked interested parties to send a not only a resume, but also a cover letter that told some things that would not normally be included on the resume. I was looking for attitude, desire, passion to work, need, and any other characteristics that might come out in such an essay.

We received about 300 replies, some of which were truly fascinating. Some were unique; some were routine; some were quite colorful; some were from people who had no resume because they had never had a job; some were from people who had had a dozen jobs in recent years. Spelling, grammar, and punctuation were all over the map, but those skills were not important to me. I was looking for an intangible—something that told me that this person would be reliable, loyal, honest, and wanted to work.

I wanted to think that I possessed a knack to ferret those characteristics out of such a letter. For the most part, I was pretty successful at identifying the applicants that fit my mold.

One idea I stressed in the interviews was that there was one phrase that I never wanted to hear from any member of the work force including myself—"It's not my job." I remembered too many instances of that attitude from the union employees in my earliest months at Kane. The very thought of a repeat of that attitude sickened me. I closely observed each candidate's reaction to that declaration. If I heard even a hint of pushback, the applicant was scratched from the list. More than a few hopefuls were disqualified on that basis.

Several applicants were in their sixties, but a real desire to work came through. One had been convicted of a non-violent crime and was on parole and doing well with his rehab. Regrets over hiring any of these people, who had been considered unacceptable by other employers in the community, were rare.

Although the plant was to be a three-shift operation, it was going to start with just one shift until we were ready to operate full scale. We called twenty people to start the first of September. At the same time, we sent letters to about a hundred others to tell them that they were on the list to be hired between late-September and the end of the year.

There was a real spirit of camaraderie among the early hires. Everyone at all levels was in the same boat in starting a new adventure in our lives. We were going to learn together and succeed or fail together. Among those twenty (half men and half women), a closeness developed that stayed with us throughout my seven years with the company. More people came and went, but there was still a special feeling among the originals.

I was eating breakfast at a restaurant in Vienna after I had been gone from Thursby for several years. Two of the women from the original team came to my table and were excited to see me. They were surprised that I remembered their names. They told me that they were still at Thursby but were continually looking for a better job. They said that the place had gone to hell after I left, and they longed for the freedom and mutual respect they had enjoyed during my tenure. I was not sure if they were being sincere or just telling me what they thought I would like to hear, but it made me feel good that they had fond memories of me and that time.

One of our early hires was Sarah Bigelow, a young woman who was slightly physically and mentally impaired. She had been in a job training program at a local agency for people with disabilities. Her letter said that the job the agency had gotten her was okay, but her case manager went with her every day and hovered over her, pointing out all of her mistakes. Because of that presence, she had not assimilated into the rest of the work force and had made no friends. I called the agency to tell them that I was hiring Sarah and that she would be part of Thursby's regular team. We would not need her case manager at any time. The woman I talked with protested. She told me, "That isn't how it works. Part of our program is the presence of the case manager."

When I let her know that Sarah's coming alone was a condition of employment, she was visibly pissed, but she backed off. Within weeks, some of the women at the plant had formed a bowling team and entered a league. Sarah was a totally accepted member of the team. The plant was sold several years ago to another plastics manufacturer. The last time I checked, Sarah was in her twenty-fourth year there.

Another thing I wasn't told in my interviews was that 100% of the Indiana customers were really pissed off over quality and lateness and were seeking another supplier. Fortunately, Thursby had a patented technology that made it difficult and expensive for a potential competitor to tool up. It would have required a major investment to serve a relatively small market. The largest customer talked about making our product internally, but apparently that idea never came to the top of their priority list.

Just a few weeks into the job, I went on a tour of the major customers with Thursby's engineering manager who was housed at the North Carolina headquarters. We intended to meet with purchasing managers, but in three of the four cases, when the CEO found out about our presence in the building, he went out of his way to impress me with his displeasure. The perception I got from the customers was far different than the story I had received from my team mates in North Carolina. The company published four-week lead times; the customers wanted one-week. I had been told that we had some orders that were "a couple weeks late". All of the customers brought out reports tracking their orders. They were getting nothing on time; the *best* Thursby did was "a couple weeks late." The norm was four to eight weeks late. They didn't want to hear that I was new on the job, and that the new plant would meet their needs. They could produce a documented history of Thursby Plastics having broken more promises than a U. S. Congressman.

Within a month after we reached full production, the plant got the tail on the late orders down to two weeks. By late-spring, we were shipping 98% on time and had reduced the announced lead-time to three weeks with an express lane that could produce a limited number of orders in a week. It took a year to make one week the standard, but we made enough gradual improvement to retain all of the customers. The quality problem was solved by simply instituting statistical process control procedures in the fabricating department. And all of this was done in a startup situation in which no experienced people were transferred from the home plant, and everyone had to be trained form the ground up.

# And Away We Go

By the first of the year, the plant had achieved its plan of being the sole producer of our product line. The management/supervision team was kept lean by using lead people for various functions. These were hourly employees who had direct or indirect jobs but who doubled in providing training and other assistance to the employees in their assigned areas. On each shift, a lead person was assigned in molding, one in fabricating, and another covered the indirect departments other than maintenance. Because maintenance was primarily done on first-shift, there was only one lead person in that area. For this additional responsibility, lead people received an extra dollar an hour. The supervisors had had up to three months to observe the competence, work habits, and attitudes of potential candidates. That made me pretty comfortable with their recommendations. It's interesting to note that seven of the ten chosen were women. That fact raised some eyebrows at headquarters, as there had never been consideration of putting a woman in charge of anything in North Carolina.

At full strength, there were about seventy people on first-shift and forty on each of the other two. Thursby was neither the top paying employer in the area nor the lowest. What we offered employees was respect, generous benefits with no co-pay, and flexibility. We allowed them to trade between shifts if someone had an occasion that she needed to be off. When orders were temporarily low, we offered *spring break days*. (It didn't matter what time of year it was; the term was constant.) These amounted to voluntary layoffs of various durations. During those times, an employee could tell his supervisor he wanted to go on spring break and schedule time off. The break could be for a specific period or indefinite. He didn't get paid, but his benefits remained intact. If orders picked up, we called those on spring break to come back to work. To retain his benefits, an employee's aggregate spring breaks could not exceed forty-five days in a calendar year.

An even more radical tactic was a program we initiated called *shove-it days*. The plant made these available at times when orders were down, but not enough to call for extended time off as in spring break days. We used these when we wanted to cut the payroll by a small amount. At these times, we played Johnny Paycheck's recording of *Take This Job and Shove It* over the intercom throughout the plant. Everyone then knew that, until the offer was rescinded, they could call in anytime up to an hour before their shift and tell their supervisor to "take this job and shove it". That meant that she would not be in today, and she did not have to give a reason. Again, she did not get paid for the day, but there was no absence marked against her. It even evolved that we offered shove-it *hours* during slack times. It was the supervisor's responsibility to juggle his work load against the people available.

Although he didn't completely fathom some of my radical ideas, the very conservative Cecil never wavered in his support. He saw the results and realized that they were spectacular. Customers were no longer calling and screaming at him. Some of the rest of the corporate management team, however, did not share Cecil's enthusiasm over Indiana's accomplishments in an area where they had failed. In particular, Dan Harwood, the controller, and Carroll Bailey, the IT manager, were beside themselves with jealousy. I was pretty sure they hit their knees every night to pray for me to fall on my ass.

Those two guys were joined at the hip. You never saw one without the other. The only thing they excelled at was incompetence. I was never able to determine which exhibited more of that, so I decided to call it a draw. In the early days of the plant, I went to Sears and opened a company account to buy a large charcoal grill. Every quarter that I was there, I cooked brats, hot dogs, and burgers for lunch for all three shifts. That meant 7 PM for second-shift and 3 AM for third. This was time well spent with the work force. People loved to see the boss serving them once in a while, since the reverse was true almost all the time.

Dan and Carroll finally got their moment when the Sears monthly statement came. Camarte had charged the company for a charcoal grill for his home. Surely, this would be a capital crime. Jerry Spade was always assigned to do anything that was potentially unpleasant because Cecil did not want to spoil his image as a man of the people. Jerry called me with a sheepish tone in his voice. He said, "Joe, I'm sure there's a perfectly good explanation for this, but I have to ask. Dan and Carroll brought me a statement from Sears that says you charged a grill to the company." I told him what it was for, and Jerry couldn't say enough about what a splendid idea that was. I didn't get to see their reaction, but I assumed that Dan and Carroll crawled back under their rock to await their next chance to torpedo me.

One of the basic duties of an accounting department is to issue monthly financial statements. In the beginning, Harwood did not want me to see the statements, claiming to Cecil that they were proprietary and on a need-to-know basis. Cecil, while a brilliant engineer, was not particularly knowledgeable about some of the other functions of the business, and he pretty much believed anything his managers told him. When Cecil told me that I would not be seeing the statements and the reason he had been given, I lost it. "Is he nuts? I've got a plant to run here, and one of the primary tools to measure of success or failure is the operating statement."

Now I had permission to see the financial statements, but only for Indiana. I didn't know until a few months later of the desperate situation in North Carolina. That information surfaced when one of the Indiana plant's resin suppliers refused to deliver except on a C.O.D. basis.

In November, after our first full month of production, I was anxiously awaiting the October financials. We were producing only 20% of our product line, but those first results were important to me. In my experience elsewhere, the monthly statements were published by the tenth of the following month. The tenth came and went; then the twentieth; finally it was December. I called Jerry Spade, who since the grill incident had become my buddy at headquarters. He told me rather casually that we never got the statements out for at least two months after the end of the month.

When I finally received the statements, sometime in January, I noticed that every number was shown in dollars and cents. Including both plants, this was a $140 million business. I couldn't imagine not rounding to thousands of dollars for purposes of the monthly statements. While I understand the need to get the balance sheet to balance, there is no value in going to the pennies level in issuing statements for the purpose of operating your business. That adds confusion and takes the focus off the relative effect of numbers that are out of line. When I asked Dan why he took this approach and didn't round his numbers to a meaningful level, he told me that nothing short of perfection was good enough for him. Furthermore, he couldn't understand why I was willing to accept sloppy reporting. What an asshole!

# Bumps along the Way

Something I learned soon after the plant got up to full production was that the people you hire to lead the startup are not necessarily the right ones to lead in the long run. You go from a level of crisis management to managing an ongoing process. While there always will be occasional bumps, your hope is that the work will become as routine as possible. The very characteristics that made our startup crew so valuable were the same ones that caused them to fail later.

Those first four supervisors were exceptional at seeing the target and running through walls, if necessary, to meet deadlines. The Indiana plant actually improved customer service during the startup of a new plant and the transfer of a product line from five-hundred miles away. There was a specific job to do, and it was amazing how quickly and effectively these guys got it done. And yet, I fired all four within two years, and every one of them agreed that he probably wasn't right to lead the ongoing operation. In fact, among them they broke most of my philosophical rules on a regular basis.

The last straws varied. One was fired for sexual harassment. Another had to go because he was a bully and showed no respect to anyone. The other two had loyalty problems. About a year into production, they cornered Cecil on one of his visits to our plant. They told him, "Joe knows nothing about manufacturing plastic products and is nothing but a score keeper and a cheer leader." When Cecil reported their comments up to me, I asked, "What's your point, Cecil?" End of discussion. These two guys were both soon gone.

As for my commitment to loyalty, we come to the greater good again. These four men, regardless of their faults, were the primary drivers of the success of the startup. And yet, it would have been self-destructive to have allowed them to continue as supervisors. In this case, loyalty amounted to giving them significantly more than the customary severance package. I arranged for that happen, and they and I moved on.

## If You Are Successful, Your Next Assignment Will Be One Where Failure is a Virtual Certainty

The success of the new plant quickly became legendary both inside the company and with customers. The Indiana people were heroes. While our plant was making money at an incredible level, the other plant was losing it even faster than we could make it.

The home plant and the headquarters were located in a rural area twelve miles south of Harper, North Carolina. Harper is an interesting small city in the western part of the state. There are several colleges and universities within a short distance. Also, the tourism business thrives in the area. These conditions give Harper somewhat of a cosmopolitan atmosphere. It is the site of more than its share of fine restaurants, unique shops, and cultural offerings.

At a national convention of plastics manufacturers in late 1990, I got Cecil aside for lunch. I told him my opinion of some of his managers in North Carolina and warned him that if they were not relieved of their responsibilities, they would fly the company into the ground. Further, at the present rate of deterioration, it would not take long for the company to become bankrupt. As brilliant an engineer as he was, Cecil was quite naive in many ways and often had trouble seeing the deficiencies in people he trusted.

My success in leading the new Indiana operation had allowed me to win Cecil's respect. I'm not sure that anyone else could have convinced him even to look at the possibility that he had misplaced his trust. Our conversation weighed on him, and after two more months of serious losses, he asked me to come to North Carolina temporarily as an internal consultant. We agreed that, starting in February 1991, I would come there three times a month for three days each time for three months. Then we would see where everything stood and make a decision for the future.

# A Carolina Christening

One of my most vivid memories began in the first five minutes on the job in North Carolina and played out over four days. Cecil had arranged for a small conference room, just off the lobby of the headquarters building, to be cleared out and furnished with a desk, a couple of chairs, and a phone. That was to be my office. The office building and the factory were separated by a courtyard about 30 yards wide. I had flown in the night before I was to start and arrived at the plant at 6:30 Monday morning. The time was chosen deliberately to coincide with the start of first-shift. At that time, the only door that was open was the factory entrance. I wore jeans and a sweatshirt, which would become my regular attire on days that I didn't meet with customers or bankers.

It had been announced that a hired gun from the Midwest was coming, but no one in the factory knew me. Several were quick to notice that there was a stranger in their midst, but they had never seen a management person in that early. Within five minutes, one of the Lubinsky brothers, Wojtek, approached me and asked if I was Joe Camarte. Wojtek and his brother Wladimir were rotational molding machine operators. Both were about 6-5 and 280. They threw those big cases around as if they were softballs. It turned out they were proud basketball season ticket holders at nearby Western Carolina University. They wanted to take me to a Southern Conference basketball game against Davidson on Thursday evening. Davidson is a frequent champion of the conference and is one of the mid-majors that usually does well in the NCAA Tournament. I told them that I would be honored. I didn't know if they wanted to make the new guy welcome or if they were just suck-ups, but I took the offer at face value. Eventually, I found the former to be true.

The Lubinskys, who were both within a year or two of 40, were the first members of their family born in America. They were life-long farmers, who still lived with their widowed mother. They raised Christmas trees on their several-hundred acre family farm. They didn't need the income they earned at Thursby, but they worked for the benefits.

I asked them to point me to the maintenance supervisor, Tom Archer. When I had toured the plant on an earlier visit, I had seen a room that did not appear to have any particular purpose. It had been a quality testing lab but had been abandoned for that purpose several months earlier. It measured about 12 x 15 feet and was located near the front of the factory. Windows along the entire front of the office allowed a view of all of the molding machines. Through the windows on the other side, I had a view of the courtyard and the office building.

I asked Tom to grab a couple of his guys and remove the few items that were in the room. I wanted them to be replaced by an old desk, a few chairs, and a six-foot round table that were stored in the back of the plant. By the time anyone from the office arrived at 8 o'clock, I was entrenched in my new office in the factory, close to the action and far removed from the other executives. That was to be my office for the nearly four years I travelled to North Carolina. Cecil and Jerry frequently encouraged me to move to the office they had established for me, but I held fast in rejecting that offer. They really never understood. I believe that that lack of understanding reflected much of the reason the company was in so much trouble.

In four days, it came time for me to accompany the Lubinskys to the basketball game. It was an early game, so we planned to go to dinner afterwards. Their season tickets were four seats in the front row of the small gym, across from the teams' benches. I don't know how big their check to the university athletic program was, but it had to be significant. Our fourth was Carl Udo, the purchasing manager. These seats were so close to the action that I felt as if someone might pass me the ball to drive in for a layup.

It was an exciting game, and at half-time the score was tied. The action had been pretty rough, and the Lubinskys had not been shy about letting their feelings about the other team and the officiating be known in their bullhorn level voices. Early in the second half, Wojtek was particularly offended by a call against the home team and was extremely vociferous in his protest. The referee was Tim Higgins, who you could see on ESPN officiating games six or seven nights a week during the season. Higgins rushed toward us to the edge of the court. That put him about eight feet from us. He called a police officer over and would not let the game resume until we were gone. The cops realized that Carl and I were innocent parties to the crime and allowed us to stay. I think they had caught the Lubinsky boys' act at previous games, but they had never been called upon to administer the equivalent of a fan's death penalty. When last seen, Wojtek was in handcuffs and Wladimir, who was not cuffed, was giving the finger to the television camera that was following the incident to its conclusion. In today's world, that would surely have been Sports Center Top-10 highlight as well as a You Tube favorite. Fortunately, Carl had driven separately and was able to take me back to the hotel. I never did get any dinner that evening.

When I arrived at work at 6:30 the next morning, Tom Archer was waiting for me at the factory entrance. He was laughing his ass off. "Have the Lubinskys offered to take you to all the games on their season tickets?" It seemed that everyone in the shop had either seen the incident on television or heard about it. The camera had taken the opportunity of the timeout to follow the procession to its end. It gave me a great story to share with my friends over a beer when I got home. I think my finding humor in that bizarre incident without seeking retribution helped with my acceptance by the work force.

## Is This What a Temp Job Is Supposed to Look Like?

The portion of the business that remained in North Carolina had sales of about $100,000,000. That plant would continue to produce shipping containers, industrial carts, outdoor storage tanks, and drums, all of which were rotationally molded. The shipping containers provided about half of the volume. Both standard and customized products were offered in the shipping container and storage tank lines. Some of the custom products, especially the shipping containers, required a high degree of engineering.

My words in describing our products to potential customers and other interested parties were, "If you need to ship, move, or store something that is so fragile or valuable that you can't risk breakage or leakage, you want to put it in a Thursby product."

Where to start? I saw three areas to attack. The first was easy to identify. It was obvious that our product offering was too fragmented for a relatively small plant to deal with efficiently. I could guess which ones were a drag on our production efficiency and profitability. However, the numbers from accounting were too unreliable to use a basis to make a decision. I decided to table that issue and concentrate on the other two problems—processes and people.

My most important staff change was to interview, Kirk Gillis, a candidate to be the new controller. At my suggestion, Cecil and Jerry hired him, and Kirk committed to start the first of June. I also recommended the firing of Dan, whom I described earlier. As a consultant, I had no real authority to order changes, but I did have strong support from Cecil and Jerry. Because they were aware of that support, most of the management team realized that it was in their best interest to implement my suggestions. However, good old Dan and Carroll remained oblivious to their shortcomings and the imminent danger they were in. Dan did not yet know that we had hired a new controller, who would start in a month.

The standard cases were assembled by installing hardware, which was either purchased or machined in-house, and foam cushioning. There were many sizes and shapes, but the assembly was pretty much the same for all.

The engineered cases were quite another story. Some of the hardware was unique to a particular design, and the cushioning was always unique. The cushioning had to be made to precise tolerances. It didn't help that, almost as often as not, the specifications that came from engineering were inaccurate. The custom cases ran over the same assembly line as the standard cases. The result was that standard cases were late because they had to wait in the queue behind custom cases.

I proffered an analogy of people trying to escape a fire through a ten-foot wide corridor if 10% of them were disabled and in wheelchairs or on walkers. If they all were to exit via the same corridor, the speed of the evacuation would be controlled by the slowest of the group. If, however, we built an interior wall within in the corridor to create a separate path for the disabled, the able-bodied could move at their own speed while the disabled would not lose any time from their maximum pace. From this example, the plant established a *special fab* line for the assembly of all the custom shipping containers. We promoted one of the senior assembly workers, who was a natural leader and had the respect of the rest of the people in the department, to be supervisor of special fab. The new line was installed in April, and it started functioning the last week I was there on the consulting job.

In the interest of simplicity, let me just say that the carts and drums created no problem in getting from raw material to finished product. That was also true of the tanks, except that the customized ones were frequently late having been held up in engineering. The carts went to a separate assembly area for the installation of hardware and wheels. For the tanks, any necessary hardware was packaged with the tank for installation by the distributor or customer.

I spent as much time as I could in an attempt to develop a closer relationship with the rest of the management team. I conducted individual and group meetings. I wanted to know what they thought—facts, opinions, suggestions, complaints, observations—about how the company did business and about relationships. They seemed uncommonly reticent, almost to the point of fright. I quickly realized that they had never been asked their opinion, and any time they had volunteered an idea, they had been ignored or even censured. The managers employed no humor in their conversations, and when I tried to lighten the mood, they didn't even smile, let alone laugh. I always thought I was a pretty witty guy. Could all of my attempts at humor not have been funny? Walking into the office building or the plant felt as if I were coming from the sunshine into a giant black cloud.

For one-on-one conversations, I went to the managers' offices. Before I sat down, I always gave them the courtesy of asking if they had time to talk with me. I told them it was okay if they were in the middle of something. I could return later at a time convenient to them. This was a level of thoughtfulness they had never seen at Thursby, and most didn't seem to know how to deal with it. In the end, three months wasn't enough time to change the expectations of managers and supervisors because they knew I would go away, and the past conditions would still exist.

By the end of April, I had fulfilled my consulting commitment. Cecil, Jerry, and I agreed that we would try handing it back to the existing management team to see if they could continue the little bit of momentum that had been established. I knew in my heart that we were hoping against hope, but I also knew that Cecil and Jerry had to come to that conclusion themselves.

I made a couple of trips back during the summer. Special fab was meeting all of my expectations, and we were catching up on orders for standard product, but the business in general was slipping away fast.

I also got with Kirk Gillis, who was only a couple weeks into his controller position, and Jerry Spade, who was Kirk's boss. I suggested that Kirk should concentrate on straightening out the accounting by product line. I admitted that because of all of the other work he had to do to deal with the mess he had acquired, this would require working some long hours. I assured him it would be worth the effort in terms of saving the company. Kirk said, "That's what I'm here for." I liked that answer.

## Here We Go Again—the Next Inherited Mess

In July, Jackie visited me in Indiana and begged me to come back to North Carolina on a full-time basis, at least until Thursby was successful in regaining profitability. He realized that the problems, if left unchecked, would eventually bankrupt the company. There was an implication that had stopped just short of a promise that I would receive stock and a significant raise plus a bonus based upon success. Jackie would see to it that his Dad appointed me executive vice president/chief operating officer. Longer term, he said that he had no interest in remaining in the business. He had other irons in the fire. As soon as the company was back on its feet, he would be moving out of the area. He planned to return only for semi-annual board meetings. If the company survived, his father would retire in two or three years, and I would become CEO.

I was well aware that, in a family business, the father and son have a right to change their minds, but I agreed to go. Because the company was suffering so much at the bottom line, I voluntarily deferred any salary increase. Cecil could make it right with me once we were making progress toward the turnaround.

By early August, I was in North Carolina indefinitely. Kate and I considered moving there but decided to delay that decision. Our daughter was entering her senior year at Vienna High School. That made an immediate relocation out of the question. Later, due to all the uncertainties that surrounded the project, we just never reached the tipping point on the decision.

One thing I have learned about taking on turnarounds of barely breathing operations is that you can hardly make a mistake. If you have any management skill at all, there will be some improvement. This would be my fourth and fifth efforts in crisis management. There had been Kane, the Thursby startup in Indiana, the business of the Indiana product line, and now I faced the Thursby plant in North Carolina and the company as a whole. The three that had been completed had all been resounding successes, but the degree of difficulty for the two at hand would be much greater. In addition, the law of averages said I was due to get hammered.

Cecil had supported my selection of Kirk as controller, but in an unthinkably soft-hearted move, he appointed Dan Harwood as manufacturing manager, where he was at least as incompetent as he had been as controller. Cecil had always been reluctant to have a plant manager, so the supervisors had loosely reported to Jerry Spade, who had so many other duties that he had to leave the supervisors pretty much on their own. The result was that there was little cooperation and much finger-pointing. Now, they would report to Dan Harwood. I never did figure out to whom he reported. As nearly as I could tell, it was nobody.

The most memorable practice Dan initiated was what I called his *double production plan*. The large customized storage containers were made on a huge rotational molding machine that required considerable time to set up, often for relatively small quantities. And frequently, there were repeat orders a few weeks later. If we received an order for ten, Dan reasoned that if we made twenty, we would not have to set up the machine again for the next order. Thirty would be even better.

There were a couple of factors that Dan didn't include in his plan. First, there was often no repeat order, and since the products were unique to a customer, we were stuck with them and ended up eating our investment of materials, labor, and overhead. Second—and this is a dandy—the only floor area that was available to store the inventory was around the fabricating line. The large containers piled up quickly to the point that if we *did* get a second order, we couldn't find the stored inventory. We ended up making new product anyway. Plus, the growing inventory hindered the fabricating workers from moving efficiently at the line. They were continually climbing over containers.

Although Kirk had stopped the counting of pennies and started getting the statements out by mid-month, he was not a magician. The numbers didn't get any better; we just knew about them sooner. It was impossible to ferret out accurate product-line results from the Dan-era books. I decided that rather than make a decision based on assumptions, we would wait until we had three months of current information before we moved on the product focus issue.

The engineering department was a black hole. The engineered orders, which were supposed to get to the floor in one to two weeks, were taking anywhere from three to twenty weeks to complete. And then they were often wrong and had to go back to the end of the line. Announced delivery time on these products, depending on the complexity, was four to six weeks. One of our biggest customers for custom containers was the defense department for shipping electronic equipment to the middle-east. Did you ever try to explain lateness of up to five months to the federal government?

The engineering manager was a good enough engineer, and he realized his department was out of control, but he had no idea how to right the ship. To exacerbate the problem, Everett Cadell, the sales manager, often shoved in a rush order, usually for a customer he was about to lose due to his inattention. Timing of IT job completions to support various facets of our work was very similar to that of engineering.

Everett Cadell had no real relationship with any major customers. He sat in his office and did business by phone. We were enlisting almost no new customers, and the old ones were bailing as fast as they could find a competitor to serve them.

Several supervisors were disrespectful of the employees. They drove their employees, rather than coaching and supporting them. Personal needs of employees were totally ignored.

I also found some positives that I should mention. The quality was pretty good—not up to 1990's standards, but returned goods were far from our biggest worry. However, we were a long way from ready for any ISO certifications that are routinely demanded of manufacturers today.

Cecil was a brilliant and innovative engineer. He sometimes contributed to the lateness by making changes after an engineer was well along in his design work. However, he was by far our best problem solver of engineering issues. And he was absolutely committed to the turnaround to the point that he allowed me to continue to call the shots.

Jerry Spade can best be described as a consummate good guy. He had no college education, but over the years he had developed considerable management ability. He had been at Thursby since the business was founded twenty-three years earlier and was as faithful as a Saint Bernard. Whatever even keel existed, Jerry deserved credit for. While his title was vice-president, the unspoken part of his job was to follow the ineffective managers and supervisors around cleaning up their mistakes. He was also invaluable as my mentor in acclimating to the company when we started the Indiana plant.

Bill Rocco, the HR manager, was the most good-hearted member of the management team. Almost to a fault, he would not hurt anyone. Cecil took considerable pride in the fact that the company had never gone through a layoff, even though there had been some hard times. Bill never resisted this policy. He was also quite competent in his specialty. He knew the laws and regulations and held the rest of us to task to comply.

Bill had one characteristic that I found humorous, but I never called him on it. Over the seven years I was with Thursby, I probably phoned him 500 times. I have a habit of asking, "How ya' doin'?" at the beginning of a phone conversation. I swear that 100% of the time Bill's answer, in a tone of resignation, was, "Oh, it's one of those days." Every time the subject came up, and he brought it up often, he told me that he worked seventy hours a week.

Let's think about what that means for a minute. If you work five days, seventy hours equates to fourteen hours a day. Add to that thirty minutes each way in transit and an hour for lunch, it's sixteen hours between leaving home and returning. If you work six days, the sixteen-hours-a-day becomes about thirteen hours. Beware of those who make these long-hour claims.

Most of them don't have a realistic concept of their time, and/or they just want to impress you with their degree of importance, commitment, or suffering.

With whatever weaknesses they had, Jerry and Bill were my only go-to guys other than Cecil in North Carolina. Bill and I had a running joke about our Italian heritage, although we were Italian in name only. In tracing our lineage back through the 19th century, neither of us could find anyone who had even been to Italy. We often joked about how we would like to come back in a future life as made men.

Now you are grounded with the knowledge of the human inventory I had to work with—some were good, but too many were inadequate. The turnaround prospects looked pretty bleak. Despite that picture, I was going to soldier on. Needless to say, I was not received with resounding joy by many when I arrived. The continuum of feelings ranged from Jerry and Bill, who accepted me with open arms, to Dan and Carroll, who were pretty sure I was going to try to hurt them and were prepared to do whatever was necessary to sabotage my efforts. I would compare their attitude toward me as similar to that of Rush Limbaugh to Barack Obama. The rest of the department heads and supervisors at least pretended to be supportive. That turned out to be true to various degrees.

That pretty well covers the situation I found after I was already committed to the long term. In keeping with the loyalty tenet of my personal philosophy, I would not quickly give up on my commitment. I knew it was time for the machete. I had pinpointed many necessary changes during my consulting gig. Now that I had the authority, I didn't hesitate to implement them when I returned.

# Time to Get Out the Machete

My first action on my first full-time day was to tell Cecil and Jerry that I was going to fire Dan and Carroll. This tested how much top-level support I would receive because it was obvious that this was an action they had resisted. They nodded and confirmed that I was in charge. I carried out my mission as soon as I left Cecil's office. I was shocked to see that Dan and Carroll were both surprised at my action. After all that had gone down, how could they not have seen this coming? An unfortunate **MACHETE MOMENT.**

Sally Cairo was second in line in the IT department and was a competent practitioner, but she had never been in a management or supervisory position. There was no conflict over not promoting her to the open department manager position. She openly declared that she was not ready and did not want to be considered. However, she did agree to take the interim lead while we searched for a permanent manager. For as long as anyone remembered, she had been the person that everyone called on for help for IT services went when Carroll had botched their jobs.

On the second day, Jonathon Gettys, senior vice-president of Commercial Bank of Charlotte called and asked me to be in his office at ten o'clock the next morning. Actually, it was more of a demand than an ask. Commercial is a huge bank with over 2 trillion dollars in assets under management. It held a $3 million dollar mortgage on the Thursby business. I had met Jonathon briefly once during my temp duty, but I didn't know him well enough to be able to anticipate his attitude. When I arrived, Jonathon was accompanied by Wynn Stroud, a partner at Tatum-Bianco, LLP, Thursby's public accounting firm. A few years later, the firm would lose its certified public accountants license. Tatum-Bianco would be found guilty of criminal charges for its handling of the audit of a major U. S. corporation that was bankrupt and would eventually cost its stockholders and creditors billions of dollars.

After about two minutes of pleasantries, Gettys opened the conversation by proclaiming, "I don't want any more of this eight-or-nine-days-a-month bullshit. You need to be here full time." The moment was reminiscent of my first meeting with Robert E over a decade earlier. He also revealed that the company had not made a loan payment in four months, and checks were bouncing like basketballs at the Final Four. The bank had been covering the checks, but he said that practice was over as of now. The bank would not have Thursby's back anymore on checks, including payroll checks. I had already been aware that Thursby was on a cash only basis with many key suppliers, but much of this was new news.

Wynn Stroud then chimed in with his expert Tatum-Bianco advice that Thursby should take a wrecking ball to the North Carolina plant and milk the cash cow in Indiana. That would probably have been the right business decision given the situation. But I rejected that idea immediately, reminding him that Cecil was committed to employment in the area and would die before he closed the plant. I negotiated a one-month grace on the check covering issue and six months to show marked improvement in the operating statement. A short leash was something I was used to from the Robert E days.

Also in the first week, I appointed Buddy Strasser, a long-time supervisor, as interim plant manager. I had been impressed with his organizational and people skills on my first tour of duty. Buddy proved to be a good choice, and he earned the dropping of the interim tag within six months. Early on, I let Buddy earn his stripes by asking him to identify the supervisors who were part of the problem and did not have the potential to be part of the solution. Then, I empowered him to fire them, which he did without hesitation. About a month later, Buddy dismissed another one, whom he had first identified as marginal.

I was getting two reputations. The management and supervision teams were scared to death of what they clearly saw as a hatchet man. Who would be the next to go? But to the people in the factory, Buddy and I were celebrities. We were getting rid of their incompetent and abusive bosses.

It was time to pick up where I had left off in regard to instilling confidence and trust in the minds of the managers and supervisors. Every Tuesday, I held a management staff meeting that included my eight direct reports. We met in my 12 X 15 office in which there were six chairs plus my desk and a round table. If you were among the last to arrive, you stood up or sat on the desk or table. Because of the windows across the front of the office, anyone who walked by could see into the meeting. That was deliberate on my part. I wanted the work of management to be as transparent as possible to those on the factory floor.

Just as had been the case at Kane, I had to get the support of the hourly work force, which numbered about 340. In the combined plant and headquarters, there were also about sixty managers, supervisors, individual contributors, and office personnel. The best way I can describe the mood in the plant and the adjacent headquarters is that it was reminiscent of the movie *Night of the Living Dead*. The people were so beaten up with failure that they were like zombies wandering through their lives.

From day-one in starting his business, Cecil had offered a quarterly profit-sharing bonus to all employees. Some quarters he gave away all of the profits in order for his employees to get a bonus, even if it was a small amount. Occasionally, a quarter was missed, usually in a recession, but never had there been the absence of a payout for three consecutive quarters. Now it had been three-and-a-half years since the last profit-sharing check. The employees weren't unwilling to work. They had been exposed to failure so much that they had totally lost confidence in the company and, even worse, in themselves.

In my second week, I started small group meetings with hourly production employees. They were invited in groups of eight. The invitation lists were random, rather than by department. I was not looking for comments on specific processes. I wanted an overview at the next level of perspective above detail. Given 320 hourly employees in the factory, my plan was to host forty meetings, and I wanted to complete them in one week. There were a total of about eighty people on second- and third-shifts. That meant that Monday through Friday I had to conduct six meetings a day on first-shift, and two or three on the off shifts. Meetings were scheduled for 45 minutes, and I gave myself a five minute break between meetings. First-shift meetings started at 7 AM, and I came back in at ten o'clock each night for the other shifts. This schedule allowed me to finish the first shift meetings by 1 o'clock each day leaving four or five hours to deal with other issues.

In some of the meetings, the participants got so wound up that the 45-minute time frame wasn't enough. In those instances, I promised to bring the group back the next week to finish. Sometimes, the second meeting would involve only one or two people, but that was okay. Those who did not return were usually satisfied with the first session.

The meetings were not mandatory. Of the eight invitees, usually six or seven showed up. I didn't ask the others why they didn't come, but I did offer makeup meetings the next week. We managed to have two full meetings of people who, for whatever reason, had not attended their originally scheduled meetings. I held the makeup meetings because I wanted to be seen as going the extra mile to allow everyone to be heard.

Much of what I learned was subjective and intangible, but I felt that most of it had value. I found the leaders, the chronic bitchers, the ones with productive ideas and positive attitudes, the ones whose attitudes would not be positive no matter what we did, and the bull-shitters. While I didn't directly follow up with a response to most of what I heard, I stored it in my memory. That information definitely influenced my subsequent actions.

The next week, I did the same thing with the non-management exempt staff and the non-exempt office employees. It turned out that, as a group, they were less forthcoming than the factory people had been. I reasoned that that was because the office employees were physically closer to those who could hurt them than the production workers were.

These meetings may have had no direct effect on solving the myriad problems the plant faced. However, I believe they instilled a particle of hope in some of the four hundred employees at Thursby Plastics' North Carolina facilities. The employees might have found someone who would listen and care about what they thought and how they felt. In that respect, I thought we had made progress.

It took a couple of months to realize fully Emerson Cadell's level of incompetence combined with his laziness, but eventually, he went the way of Dan and Carroll. I promoted our top salesman, Ted Danvers to sales manager. Ted turned out to be perfect for the job.

Despite whatever gain we had achieved from the meetings, by mid-September I was pretty distraught. I had been home only once in six weeks. The bank had indicated they were not going to be very patient. The situation often appeared to be hopeless. I had no social life or contact with people away from the plant. There had been a few dinner invitations from some of the managers, but I had been deliberate in declining them. Because of the uncertainty of the future, both for the company and individuals, I made it a policy not to get close to anyone. I was determined to be friendly but not familiar. Plus, when I left the office, I needed to get away completely.

# A Load *off* My Mind

With the completion of the September operating statement (delivered on October 9, by the way), we were able to make an easy decision about which product lines to keep. The storage tanks were clearly our biggest loser. There were many short runs, and our engineers had to fit design projects for them into their schedules almost as an afterthought. We just could not give the product the attention it needed.

Suzy Carpenter, one of our best young engineers had told us for some time of her dream to start her own business. We asked her if she wanted to manufacture storage tanks. We would give her the business and, for a fair price, would sell her a rotational molding machine that would become expendable to us. Suzy had spent a little time working on that product for us and was eager to take it if she could make the necessary arrangements. I told her she could take whatever time off she needed in order to pursue the opportunity. In about a month, she had her financing lined up and a building rented. We quickly closed the deal, and Suzy was in business in her small factory on the other side of Harper. About two years later, I ran into her in Harper. She had gotten out of the highly competitive stock storage container business and had established a specialty custom line. She employed a work force of ten people and had carved out a profitable niche business.

# And a Load *on* My Mind

One Saturday evening in late-September, I found myself in my hotel room wallowing in self-pity. I had not even been going out to dinner, choosing instead to pick up deli meat, bread, and chips, which I ate in my room each evening. I realized that I needed do something to get out of the funk I was in, so I decided to go into town. I had seen ads for The Devlin Music Hall, a club type venue in downtown Harper that featured an eclectic mix of live music, including occasional national and regional name acts.

This night, Vance Gilbert, a singer-songwriter from Boston was appearing as part of his east coast tour. As a party of one, I was seated with another single, a man named Bob. As far as I know, Bob didn't have a last name, nor did I to him. He was about my age and readily told me that had been estranged from his son for two years and that his wife had kicked him out three months ago. Further, this was the first time he had been out of his rented room, other than to go to work, since the separation. What a coincidence—two losers found each other in the night. Sometimes, you need a complete stranger to whom to express your innermost thoughts.

Bob was an alumnus of nearby Mars Hill College and had been to their football game that afternoon. I didn't know Mars Hill had a football team, but apparently it does. I sensed that going to the game had helped him realize that there might be life after divorce.

Vance Gilbert was outstanding. His songs ranged from humorous to poignant and, as a whole, were quite uplifting. His music, coupled with his delightful personality, buoyed my spirits for the first time in weeks. Putting that together with Bob's sad tale and the sense that he might be on the verge of bouncing back, made me feel that maybe I didn't have it so badly after all—that there were still some good things in life. I just needed to look for them and recognize them when they came.

At the time, I didn't tell Kate this story because I had not told her how down I was. She had enough to do holding down the fort at home and getting our youngest daughter ready to go to college.

However, that winter on a rare visit home, I read that Vance Gilbert was going to appear at a club about thirty miles from home. I then related my story to Kate and told her that I would like to go. She was quick to agree. Kate wanted to grab onto anything that would help her relate to what I was going through. Vance again gave an outstanding performance. During his break between sets, I caught up to him and told him of the profound effect he had had on my life. He seemed to listen intently and commented about how, as a performer, you rarely know how you affect individuals in your audience. We chatted for about five minutes and wished each other well. I don't know if the story was at all important to Mr. Gilbert, but thanking him for providing me with a small life affirming experience made me feel better.

# Is It Possible to Clean and Think in the Same Day?

By mid-October, I figured it was time for my next move in empowering the people. Each step in this change of culture was extremely threatening to the middle managers and supervisors. However, Cecil, Jerry, and Bill remained supportive no matter how over-the-top some of my actions were.

I subscribe to a theory that housekeeping in a factory is an indicator of quality, productivity, on-time delivery, morale, and usually, profitability. And this place was a real dump.

I called a meeting of managers and supervisors at four o'clock in the afternoon on a Monday in early October to inform them of my plan for the next morning. The forecast was for a beautiful Carolina fall day with a high temperature of 74 degrees. I had waited until the day-shift hourly work force was gone so that the activities to come would be a surprise. All of the supervisors were to report no later than 6 AM, a half-hour ahead of the hourly people.

The purchasing manager was to make a trip to Home Depot that evening and buy a large supply of brooms, mops, and other cleaning materials to bring in the morning. The supervisors were told to scatter many of the larger containers, those Dan had made through his double production strategy, throughout the plant. Others were assigned to bring doughnuts, coffee, soft drinks, and ice.

It's relevant to note that Cecil had a strict rule against the playing of music in the office and plant. In addition, he absolutely abhorred rock-and-roll, claiming that it was the root of the deterioration of society. That afternoon, I briefed him with an overview of my plan. I told him that a '50's rock-and-roll mix tape that I had made especially for this occasion was an essential component of the activities. Cecil cringed, but he didn't say no. He realized that I was informing him, not asking permission, and he appeared to appreciate the heads-up.

Morning arrived, and all of the team was there with their items as assigned. The weather was as promised. It was quite cool, and there was a fog rising from the wooded area in the distance. I then understood the term *Smoky Mountains*. It was obviously going to be a beautiful day. The employees arrived and went to their work stations, as usual. There was a paging system throughout the plant that was tied to the phones. At 6:35, I dialed into the system and started the tape on a portable cassette player placed beside my phone. The first track was Chuck Berry singing *Roll over Beethoven*. People stopped in their tracks. It looked as if they thought they had passed into the *Twilight Zone*. I let the tape play for five minutes uninterrupted. Then I paused the recording and got on the PA. I asked everyone to stop their work and meet me in the courtyard in ten minutes. As they gathered, the sun was just beginning to appear above the east horizon, but there was enough of a morning glow to make out the shapes of the workers.

I climbed up onto one of the several wood picnic tables in the courtyard to address the group. The 260 first-shift factory employees, managers, and supervisors were gathered. I told them that their surroundings were disgusting and that they were going to spend the next three hours to clean up as much as possible in that short time. Then they were to meet me back in the courtyard at 10 AM. At 8:30, when all the office people had arrived, they were informed of the 10 AM gathering.

Most of the employees really seemed to enjoy the assignment. I left the tape on with its never-ending supply of Jerry Lee Lewis, Fats Domino, the Big Bopper, and others of that era and genre. Of course, there was plenty of Elvis—but only his early, ground-breaking material—none of that *In the Ghetto* and *My Way* crap. All of the tracks were fast to set a pace for the work at hand. A few people even danced while they worked. It wasn't quite a scene from *Grease,* but it was joyful. Supervisors oversaw the cleanup in their regular areas. The managers loaded snacks and drinks onto carts and moved through the shop, delivering treats to those who were cleaning. It was a big deal to have the formerly untouchable managers serving the people for a change. It appeared that half of them had never been in the factory and did not know even one of their team mates who made the products that provided their livelihood.

At 9:45, I went on the intercom again to say that it was time to finish what they were working on. They had fifteen minutes to wash up and get to our meeting in the courtyard. Bill Rocco had divided the work force into groups of about twelve people each. That made for about twenty teams. This time, people in the same department were kept together. Office non-exempt employees were included. For small departments such as purchasing and accounting, people were combined into one group.

I read the names assigned to each group and asked that they gather as teams around my table. When all the groups were formed, they were each given a flip-chart each and several colored markers. Their task was to decide on a problem or an opportunity for their team to discuss. Then they were to develop some ideas relevant to their subject. The subject could be a suggestion for improving productivity or quality, suggestions about process flow, or anything other issue of mutual interest to the members of the group. Personal attacks, such as "our supervisor is an asshole", were declared out of bounds. If a group finished all it had to say on its first issue, it could identify a second.

Each team was advised to elect a facilitator from within their ranks. This person's job was to keep the conversation moving—not to be in charge. The group was also to select a scribe, who would record their comments and suggestions on the flip chart and act as timekeeper. I asked them to work through their normal lunch break with the promise that the managers would deliver pizza and cold drinks to their chosen work site. A few had errands to run at lunch and were excused to do so. All groups were to bring their flip charts and meet me back in the courtyard at two o'clock.

Engineers, accountants, and other exempt personnel would be available for consultation. Managers and supervisors would be roaming the grounds to answer questions but were instructed to keep their distance unless invited in. They were forbidden from eavesdropping or becoming part of the group.

The sun was up by now, and the temperature was in the low 60's. Those mountain folk are a pretty hearty lot, so many teams decided to meet outside. Some went into the office and some into the plant. As I walked around, I could see that, almost to a person, they were taking the work seriously. Several didn't even notice me walking by, or if they did, they didn't look up. After all, this was their opportunity to have an influence in righting some of the wrongs they had seen for years.

At two o'clock, everyone reassembled. I asked each facilitator to come to the picnic table and tell the crowd the issue(s) her team had discussed. I didn't want detail. I just wanted everyone to see the variety of topics that were important from various perspectives. I was not disappointed. While there were several duplications, there was enough variety to show the magnitude of the work we had in front of us.

I repeated a scaled down version of the exercise on the smaller second and third shifts. Most of the housekeeping work on those shifts consisted of cleaning out what had become known as Dan's folly—the huge pile of unused containers. The night supervisors again oversaw the work, and I was the delivery boy for food and drinks. The expert consultants from management weren't there, but I took questions, and if I couldn't answer them, I promised to check tomorrow and come back with the answer. That was the last all-nighter I was ever to pull in my career. An all-night **MACHETE MOMENT.**

I had committed that I would review and evaluate all the flip charts as soon as possible and report back to the work force. I used the next day to do a quick read of all of the comments. There were quite a few entries that I didn't understand. Over the remaining two days of that week, I tracked down the facilitator or a team member for a clarification of those that confused me. By the end of the week, I knew what had been said and meant. I went home to Indiana that weekend, and spent several hours identifying and grouping comments that appeared on multiple reports. Kate was less than happy that I took a significant portion of our rare time together to work, but she understood. When I had reviewed all of the comments, I found there were 143 unique ideas, suggestions, and complaints. Over a hundred of them, which we labeled "quickies," were so simple that they could be implemented in minutes. Just because an item was a quickie did not mean that it couldn't be an *A*.

On Monday, still at home, I prioritized the 143 items as *A*, *B*, and *C* urgency. There were eight that I listed as irrelevant or undoable and explained why I had reached that conclusion in my report. The remaining 135 were each assigned to a manager to develop an action plan with a due date. He was then responsible to use the necessary resources to bring the project to fruition by the due date. Any changes in the scope or completion date had to be approved by me. I kept about twenty items for myself.

When I returned to North Carolina on Tuesday, I called a management meeting to share the list. I had already assigned each item to a specific manager. Each received an even mix of *A*'s, *B*'s, and *C*'s, and each had the opportunity to make his case for an item to be reassigned to a different manager or from another to himself. There were only a handful of such requests, all of which made sense and were accepted. We changed the priority rating up or down on a few others and combined some for which I had not seen the connection. The meeting was adjourned with agreement as to how we would address the list.

Based on the agreed upon list, I issued a report to all employees. It included a brief description of the problem/suggestion, its priority code, and the name of the manager responsible so that everyone would know who was accountable. This was a real building block in establishing management's credibility with the employees. They were amazed that we had responded so quickly and thoroughly.

In the ensuing weeks and months, the managers knocked off the items one by one. A natural part of coming to a solution was that the manager almost always had to consult with one or more hourly employees. As we proceeded, some of the 135 became unnecessary because conditions changed due to the successful completion of a higher priority item.

The suggestions ranged from changing the way we communicated between engineering and the factory floor to several changes in both container assembly lines. After six months, a report was issued to all employees that showed items that hadn't been completed. If necessary, a revised due date was included.

One excellent suggestion was to fire-sale the hundreds of overrun containers, first to employees and then to charities and individuals in the community. While none of them had any cushioning, and many had no hardware, they were perfect to use for storage in garages or basements. First, we gave the employees three days to buy anything they wanted in a silent auction format. Then we put the word out to the community as to the process and dates of the open sale. This was a great example of the win-win concept. Much of the space that had been cluttered by cases we couldn't use was cleared. And Thursby Plastics established goodwill with employees, citizens, and charities for giving them something that would be useful to them for little or nothing.

Another suggestion was to communicate better with the employees as to the progress the company was or was not making toward survival. The reasoning was that their livelihoods were on the line, and they should know where we stood. That made perfect sense, and we implemented the suggestion immediately on all shifts.

A carryover from the pre-Camarte days was the conducting of employee informational meetings. These were held quarterly and were optional and not well attended. The people realized that the information shared was not substantive. The suggestion clearly called for information that had previously been considered confidential. I believe Dan had set the standard for confidentiality, and he had wanted to keep virtually everything to himself.

This was a time of crisis. If we wanted our employees to participate in solutions, we needed to share all the information and answer all the questions we reasonably could. To separate this program from the former failed meetings, I called them *people meetings,* instead of employee meetings and scheduled them monthly, rather than quarterly. I thought this connoted more of a feeling that we were in this turnaround together. The lunch room could seat about sixty people, so we split those who worked in the daytime into several sessions. There was one meeting for each of the other shifts. I personally hosted every meeting and shot straight from the hip. I shared the good news and the bad news with equal candor. Cecil spoke briefly but passionately at the first-shift meetings. The cleanup event had been clearly a test of my Collective Brainpower theory, and it had passed with flying colors.

# I Didn't Sign On for This, But Things Have a Way of Working Out

From my first trip to the area for my original interview, I had always stayed at the Anthony Inn, which was about two miles south of the center of Harper. It was adequate, but not exceptional. I resisted going to town at night because I didn't want to drive after drinking. Occasionally, I went in for dinner and limited myself to two beers, but I didn't do that often. A few times, when someone such as Charmaine Neville, Maria Muldaur, or Terence Blanchard was appearing, I went to the Devlin Music Hall. But that was only once every few weeks and when Kate visited.

One night, after about six months as a faithful, paying guest of the Anthony Inn, I went into the hotel bar for a nightcap with a Tatum-Bianco consultant with whom he I become friends. We had been to dinner in town, so it must have been about 10 o'clock. We sat at the bar of the half-filled room and had a couple of beers. As far as I could see, nothing noteworthy was happening in the room. I got turned on by the smell of the popcorn that was popping in a microwave behind the bar. I asked the bartender if he would fix a batch for us. He had served us in a normal way without being particularly friendly or unfriendly. That was okay; I had a friend for the evening and didn't need another. When he wasn't making drinks, the bartender talked with a couple that he appeared to know a few stools down from us.

After about fifteen minutes, I was ready for another beer and realized that we had never gotten any popcorn. I ordered a round with a hand gesture and asked how our popcorn was coming. There might have been a bit of a wise-ass tone in my question, but it was said good-naturedly with a smile, and I certainly was not abusive. The bartender went into a rage and started screaming at the top of his voice, "You fat fuck, I'll show you how your popcorn's coming. I'll kick your ass." And he started around the bar.

I admit that I was a little overweight, but I was in pretty good shape at that time. I kind of thought he might have trouble carrying out his threat of kicking my ass, but I really didn't want to test him. By the time he reached me, a waiter and some customers were holding him back, and all we had was a shouting match. The hotel night manager, who appeared to have no authority, took me into the lobby to apologize. The bartender went back to work behind the bar.

I remember a few outcomes of that memorable moment, none of which strengthened my loyalty to the Anthony Inn. The bartender never apologized. There was a basket of cheap fruit in my room when I came in the next evening. I guess management thought that would make us even. It did not. When I mentioned the incident to the general manager the next day, she said, "Those things happen sometimes." The bartender was never censured in any way. We weren't even comped for our bill. My friend paid the check. I don't know if he left a tip. And most important, we never did get any popcorn.

I'm not sure if it was a result of the incident or a coincidence, but a week or two later, I was contacted by the manager of the Hotel Americaine. The Americaine was located in downtown Harper and had been a local landmark since 1932. The publicity materials stated that it had been host to such notables as Lyndon Johnson, Paul McCartney, Harrison Ford, Eleanor Roosevelt, and the Dalai Lama. The manager was offering a deeply discounted rate for all of my stays if I would steer visitors to Thursby her way. I told her that I would make suggestions to visitors, but I could not guarantee their acceptance. That was good enough for her to make the deal. Now, they could add Joseph P. Camarte to the list of notables on their Website.

In the early nineties, the going rate at the Hotel Americaine was about

$150 a night. I paid twenty bucks for each of 200 nights a year for over two years. Good deal! Finally, a hotel auditor realized what was happening and raised my special rate to $60. That was still a good deal. Not only were these accommodations luxurious and much more comfortable than the Anthony, they put me within walking distance to Nat's Saloon.

Nat's was my version of Cheers. The bartenders quickly befriended me, and I became an every-night customer. My friendship with the bartenders, Jack, Buck, and Rog, grew to the point where we got past bar talk to news of each other's families and other personal interests. Before long, I had a fairly large support group of bartenders, staff, the owner, and a covey of regular barflies—not an elite lineup, by some standards, but exactly what I needed to lift me from the depths, at least some of the time.

Virtually every night I was in town, the regimen was the same regardless of the weather, time, how tired I was, or what was on my mind. I parked in the hotel lot and walked directly to Nat's. This was my therapy. I took Kate there to meet my friends when she visited about three times a year. I could see her eyes roll, but she was glad that I had managed to find some degree of contentment to relieve the stress. I took some twisted form of pride in being the only non-employee invited to the Nat's annual company holiday party on the first Monday or Tuesday of January. Kate and I even went to Jack's wedding. I played golf on two or three occasions with Jack and Buck. Rog was a full time middle-school teacher in an adjoining town. At his invitation, I spoke twice at the school's career day. Jack recommended a couple of his friends who were looking for work. I interviewed them for factory jobs on Nat's barstools and hired them. I understand that one of them recently received his twenty year award.

# There's a First Time for Everything

While the internal signs—quality, productivity, morale, my credibility—were improving, the ones that really mattered to the bank were still ugly. I was certain that the improvements would soon become visible on the operating statement, but would it happen soon enough?

On New Year's Eve 1991, just as Kate and I were preparing to go out to dinner, I received a call from Cecil. He, Jackie, Bill Rocco, and Kirk Gillis, had gone into panic mode without consulting me. They had been together for ten hours. What they had come up with to solve Thursby's financial woes was to put everyone on short hours and reduce their pay proportionally. Of course, exempt employees would be expected to work their regular hours, albeit one day a week would be gratis. This would apply to everyone in the organization. I admit that my knee-jerk reaction was selfish. I wasn't going to endure all this pain *and* take a pay cut.

But the selfish interest was just the tip of the iceberg in all that was wrong with their plan. The plant had almost caught up with orders for two reasons. (1) Some of the changes we made were taking effect and productivity was improving, and (2) demand had fallen off considerably, especially from the government, due to the end of Desert Storm several months earlier. A decrease in demand is not the best way to catch up when you are hopelessly behind, but it did make the task a little easier.

Cecil had always been proud to tell one and all that his company had never experienced a layoff. While that is commendable, it is not always the best approach from a business standpoint. My contention was that when you reduce everyone's hours and pay, you piss off *everyone*. When you remove a number of employees who are not needed at the moment, the remaining ones are grateful that they still have jobs. And especially in a non-union environment, you can use the opportunity to get rid of deadwood, of which Thursby Plastics had more than its share. And you stop paying benefits to those who are permanently gone.

I considered replicating the spring break and shove it days we used in Indiana. In the end, I decided that would be too drastic of a change for both the supervisors and employees in North Carolina to handle. Maybe another time.

I told Cecil not to do anything until I got there. Having hastily made travel arrangements, I flew on New Year's Day to North Carolina and was in Cecil's office when he got there on the morning of Tuesday, January second. I showed Cecil and Bill Rocco the layoff plan I had drafted on the plane. It included 65 factory hourly, eight office non-exempt, and fifteen exempt employees. Of these, 38 people were to be permanently terminated, and fifty would retain the right to be recalled. The fifty would also keep their benefits for up to six months if they chose to remain on the recall list. Those who were terminated would receive a week's pay for each full year of service and would retain their company paid insurance benefits for two months. They would also keep both the company's and their own contributions to the 401-k plan. Any of the fifty with recall rights could waive that opportunity and receive the same package as those terminated. Cecil was distraught at setting this precedent, but he relented and seemed to understand why this method was better. I suggested that he not come in the next day so that he could be buffered from the process. He appreciated that consideration and complied.

Bill and I spent the rest of that day preparing the hit list, which was based on a combination of seniority, competence, and attitude. We called the managers and supervisors together first thing Wednesday morning to share the plan and the list with them. The managers and supervisors had the opportunity to make a case to change the list, but I gave them to understand that the number was fixed. By the end of a difficult three-hour meeting, we had settled on how many and who. Actually, it went pretty well, and in the end, the supervisors had increased the number by two. Everyone was instructed to leave the meeting room and execute the plan immediately. The terminations were to be done first. The supervisors and managers were to report back to me when each was finished.

By two o'clock, everyone had been notified, and those affected were out the door. A few of them stopped by Bill's office or mine on their way out. Most said they felt disappointed but realized it needed to be done and thought the procedure was fair. The off-shift supervisors met with the few affected employees on second and third shifts as they entered the plant that evening.

## All Families Have Some Quirks—the Thursbys Are No Exception

By summer 1992, day-to-day activities seemed to have become pretty much routine. I noticed that Cecil's wife Elvina had become more of a presence in my life. I had met her on several occasions, and I knew that she came into the office a couple days a week to work on some of her charitable causes. I found her to be a pleasant person to talk with. Elvina was in her sixties and was somewhat of a unique character. I had heard that she came from wealth; her father had been ambassador to some small island nation. She was a pretty woman who wore her hair in a tight bun. I'm no fashion expert, but her choice of clothing reminded me of the schoolmarm on *Little House on the Prairie.*

I never thought that she wanted anything to do with the business. And yet, she kept showing up at my office for no apparent reason. In time, I realized she was trying to bring peace to her family, and she thought that I could be a catalyst in that effort. Little by little, she let me know how strained the relationship between Cecil and Jackie had become. Of course, the personal disagreements were fueled by the unstable state of the business. She was certain that, if the cause could be repaired, harmony would be restored. Jackie was in his early thirties and was temporarily living at home. Elvina openly wept as she described the soap opera that was her home life. Cecil was hanging on by his fingernails to continue to be in charge, and Jackie was insisting that he unconditionally turn everything over to me as the only hope of saving the company.

In October 1992, Bill Rocco set up a lunch meeting for Cecil, Jackie, and me to visit John Temple, the owner of a manufacturing business in a neighboring town. Mr. Temple had reached a point with his company that was similar to Cecil's. He was an entrepreneur who had started a business that outgrew his management acumen. He had gone outside his family to hire a professional manager and had turned all operations over to him. John remained board chair, but his involvement was from the 30,000-foot level.

Mr. Temple extolled the virtues of stepping away from the day-to-day operation of the business. He decided to allow a professional, who was extremely competent and whom he trusted implicitly, to deal with those headaches. He strongly advised Cecil that, if he had found such a person, he should make the same move. John told Cecil that the change would allow him to relax and enjoy life. What none of those advising him realized, or maybe just didn't face up to, was that Cecil had few interests outside his business. It seemed that it was sometimes distressing for him to leave work at night.

On the ride home, Cecil was still resistant, and Jackie was still persistent. No meeting of the minds had been reached when we arrived back at the office. There were a couple of months of procrastination before Cecil finally relented as Bill Rocco finally pushed my promotion to the finish line. Even then, it was apparent that Cecil was not comfortable with the outcome. I think he was just tired of Jackie's constant badgering.

In January 1993, I was appointed executive vice-president/chief operating officer. I also received a decent raise. I was still underpaid compared to others in the same position in similar organizations, but I was okay with that. Money is not my primary motivator, and considering that we were still struggling, the company really could not afford any more. The last thing I wanted was to be part of the problem.

Elvina continued to visit a couple times a month. It appeared that I was her only confidante. I always listened without saying much. I felt that my position regarding the Thursbys' family issues was a lot like one might experience when a couple splits up, and the guy tells you what a bitch his wife is. Don't ever weigh in on that comment because inevitably they will get back together, and he will hold it against you that you called his wife a bitch. And probably, he will tell her so that she can hate you too. I was aware of the strengths and weaknesses in both of Elvina's men, and there was no point in my commenting on them. So I commiserated, occasionally offering a benign word of advice.

In addition, she was almost gushing in her thanks to me for supporting the men in her life and for saving their business. I responded that she was a bit premature in that it hadn't been saved yet. But we were on the upswing, and I appreciated her expression of gratitude. She gave me full credit for the improvement, which is never quite deserved. While something like that is always a team effort, it would not have happened without me or someone like me to lead it. There are probably a million men and women out there who could have done what I did, but the original cast of characters at Thursby Plastics would never have succeeded.

# A Little Sunshine Peeking Through the Dark Clouds

As winter ended in 1993, the plant was in better condition—not good, but better than horrible. The company had turned a profit in the fourth quarter of 1992. Deliveries of the standard product line were nearly 100% on time, and rejections due to quality problems were next to nothing. Thursby Plastics was not overdrawing its checking account and actually could buy on credit from most suppliers.

Jonathon Gettys at the bank, while not effusive in his praise, was at least nodding in approval that we seemed to be recovering. Thursby had not caught up on back loan payments, but we were consistently paying the current month on time. However, Gettys just couldn't let it go with unqualified approval. He had to add some bullshit about not counting our chickens. It was obvious that he thought our team had been more lucky than good to this point. I'm still not sure he was wrong. It was evident that he would be surprised if the improvement continued.

The main remaining negative was that designs for special products were still shipping late. I looked at data from the special fab line and watched the employees in action. They were functioning efficiently enough to exonerate themselves from the conclusion that they were a significant part of the problem. Then I looked at the engineering records. When were orders released to the floor? When did they get to special fab? How often did they have to go back to have errors corrected? It wasn't a pretty picture. Less than a 25% of orders were being delivered on time to the purchasing and rotational molding departments, and 40% had to go back to be reworked because it was impossible to assemble the case as it was designed. The elimination of the storage tank line should have given some relief, but that did not appear to have transpired to any great degree.

The layout of the engineering department was such that the manager worked in an enclosed office. All of the engineers and drafters were seated in six-foot high cubicles. I had heard from several sources that they spent much of their time in their cubicles reading magazines, playing computer games, and having personal phone conversations. I really don't like snitches, but I felt an obligation to check out this accusation. Sure enough, a little snooping on my part corroborated what I had heard.

Here was another machete moment right in front of me. I was angry that, while the rest of the work force at all levels was busting ass to recover, these guys were fucking off. Actions carried out in anger are akin to going to the grocery store when you are hungry. You throw moderation to the winds. Late one April day, I called Tom Archer, the maintenance supervisor, to my office. I told Tom that I wanted him to bring three of his men to my office as soon as they arrived the next day. I would instruct them at that time as to their assignment, but they should plan to be on the project for the entire morning.

When the time came, I told them to go to engineering and rip out every one of those cubicles leaving only the manager's office and an open area where we could put individual desks. The work was well underway by the time the engineers began arriving about 8:30. It won't surprise you to learn that they were livid. They demanded to know from Tom why this was happening and who was responsible. I went to meet with the department employees about 8:45, when I was sure they would all be there, and admitted responsibility.

The engineers were still in the dark as to how to deal with me, so they refrained from the violent reaction that I knew was inside them. However, they were clearly pissed, which they should have been. I had intended to get their attention, and I had succeeded. One fact I had not realized caused me to have some egg on my face. All of their electrical connections were embedded in the cubicles, and the cubicle walls were lined with pictures of their families or whatever was dear to them. By early afternoon, they had retrieved all of their pictures, and the electricity was hooked up so they could function. Some of the work surfaces had been connected to the cubicle walls. Maintenance replaced those with desks and file cabinets they had in storage and filled in with some folding tables we bought at Target. Eventually, the company bought new furniture for the department.

I also instructed the engineering manager that I wanted his door open at all times so that he could see what was going on in his department. I was also holding him responsible to see that, within two months, the department was 90% on time with no more than 10% returns from the shop floor. Then we would review and possibly tighten those standards. I flew back to Indiana that afternoon after stopping at a pay phone at the airport to order a dozen roses to be sent to the department. I heard later that the roses ended up in the trash can upon receipt, but I didn't care. I had made my point, and in less than two months, the department was meeting the standards I had set. In retrospect, this was a **MACHETE MOMENT** for which I was pleased with the result but was not proud of the method.

When I look back, I know that I had been too impetuous in swinging the machete and had taken too great a risk. I also know that, whether because of or despite my action, the problem got solved. Again, I was lucky that it worked out. Thanks, Lou.

Despite my own misgivings, much of the work force outside engineering had been aware of the slacker attitude in this vital department and applauded my action, which became known as Jericho day. None of the engineers shared the humorous point of view of the event.

I don't always rejoice in machete moments. I rue the fact that they are ever necessary, but when they are, I feel that I need to be relentless and swift in the execution of them. I have also learned that I need to be careful not to be excessive in the use of my power. The case could be made that sometimes Machete Moments appear to violate the Golden Rule. However, to have avoided taking action would have ignored the concept of the greater good. The consequence of inaction could have been disastrous. The jobs of the other 550 people in two states, who depended on Thursby's success in order to feed their families, would have been put at greater risk than they already were.

When do you cross the line between truth and rationalization? That's one question that, no matter how late into the night I stew over past actions, I've never able to answer to my satisfaction. Balancing the Golden Rule against the greater good is an art that I'm not sure anyone has mastered. I know I haven't.

Three of the engineers ended up as casualties over the next few months because their productivity was low and their attitudes were unacceptable reflecting a grudge over the incident. But their attitudes were lousy before their walls were torn down.

I could finally see that we had a chance to save Thursby Plastics. By late spring, demand had increased, and the company had recalled almost all of the employees who had been laid off. I thought we needed one more visible impetus. At the June people meeting, I told the old story of the chicken and the pig. As I often do when speaking to groups, I drew stick figures to represent various points. For this meeting, I drew a plate of bacon and eggs and beside it a chicken and a pig. If there are two or three of you reading who have not heard this old motivational chestnut, it goes like this:

"I had bacon and eggs for breakfast today. I have a chicken and a pig to thank for that meal. The chicken was involved in providing it, but the pig was committed." The punch line of course was, "I want all of you to be like the pig." The story drew a few chuckles after which I asked everyone, including Cecil, to stand and raise his right hand and repeat after me.

"I am committed to doing my part in returning Thursby Plastics to its past level of success. I am committed to work hand-in-hand with my fellow associates to achieve this success. I AM A PIG!"

As silly as this exercise seemed, not only did the majority of the people tolerate it, they were euphoric in their reception of it. It was somehow meaningful to them as a touchstone of solidarity that symbolized hope for the future. Cecil thought this was one of the funniest things he had ever seen. His joy was boundless, and he didn't stop laughing for three days. He even added it to his repertoire of oft-told tales.

After the recall, we had left third-shift with a skeleton crew of five men. I came in at 5:30 in the morning on the first Tuesday of each month to host their people meeting. At this meeting, I still told the story, but I thought it might be awkward or embarrassing to ask such a small group to take the pledge, so I said we could dispense with that if they wished. However, they had heard about it from friends on previous shifts and insisted on taking it. They wanted to show me that they were as dedicated as those who were more part of the day-to-day action.

A woman who worked on the fabricating line was an artist. She volunteered to design tee shirts, which we had made and passed out to every employee. They read, "I'm proud to work for Thursby Plastics. I'M NOT CHICKEN TO BE A PIG." She illustrated them with line drawings of a chicken and a pig. Most people wore those shirts to work at least once a week, and, occasionally, I would see one when I went to the grocery store. I took this whole experience as a reminder that no matter how dire the circumstances, it doesn't hurt to include a little fun and humor in the rehabilitation process. I made a big deal about the employee who designed the shirts. The voluntary collaboration with management by a production employee was symbolic. A **MACHETE MOMENT.**

# I Needed Some Managers I Could Count On

I had become anxious about the lack of depth in the plant's leadership ranks. The managers and supervisors that remained were generally adequate, but most were not outstanding. I thought that, with most, it was more that they were conditioned to mediocrity, rather than a lack of competence. Nevertheless, I needed to get some people I could rely on to think innovatively and act decisively. That meant calling on people whose character, work ethic, loyalty, and intelligence I already knew.

In May 1993, the sales manager (actually the only salesman) for our Indiana products retired. He had been skating through the job for some time, but he had a good personal relationship with most of the customers. What he didn't have, however, was their confidence that he could resolve lead time, delivery, and quality problems.

Bill Muldoon was an old tennis buddy of mine who had been an engineer at Denard. He had been caught in one of their big downsizings two or three years earlier and had established a one-man business, which might have been turning a small profit. I called him from North Carolina early on a Saturday morning to ask him if he would like to become Thursby's sales manager for Indiana products. He would not have to move from his Vienna home. Without asking about salary, benefits, or job requirements, he said yes. He told me jokingly that if hadn't gotten a real job soon, his wife was going to kick him out of the house.

Bill did an outstanding job. The product, compared to those he worked on at Denard, was simple. He had a handle on it after a few days with our engineers in North Carolina and our production crew in Vienna. The customers soon came to respect him because he could communicate their issues back to the plant, and their problems got solved. That is not a unique practice but one that so many, including his predecessor, did not understand.

My son, Jeff, was two years out of business school at Indiana University and was working in sales for another plastics company in the Charlotte area. I introduced him to Ted Landers in the hope that Ted would see his qualities and hire him as a sales rep. I realized that it would have been difficult for Ted to reject hiring my son into an open job, but potential accusations of nepotism were the least of my worries. Jeff was 23, single, and lived in an apartment, so he traveled light. In June 1993, he was able to move all of his possessions to Harper in his car in one trip.

Another old friend, Rick Pierce, was an engineer with whom I had worked and played flag football in the late-sixties. He had gravitated into marketing halfway through his career and had done quite well. He and I lost track of each other for a decade in the seventies but had gotten back together in 1983. We had seen each other a couple of times a year and had talked often since then. In that time, Rick and I had become almost brotherly in our friendship. He had retired at age 45 to putter with his own various business interests. At my request, a friend of mine in Vienna invited him to his Super Bowl party in 1994. There he and I spent a great deal of time chatting. I had a more serious motive than watching a football game in wanting Rick to come two hundred miles from his home in Columbus, Ohio.

I was considering buying a business with a unique product for Thursby's North Carolina plant. I asked Rick if he would go with me to eastern Kentucky, as a consultant, to meet with the owner and look at the business. Upon seeing the operation, we both agreed that it was a good deal and that it would be a good fit for the North Carolina operation. It could be absorbed into our existing processes without interrupting production and had the potential to add to the bottom line. I thought Thursby Plastics might be in good enough standing with the bank by this time that we could borrow the $200,000 needed for the purchase.

I wanted to get Rick committed before I went to Cecil. I asked Rick if he would be willing to come on board to manage the startup if this deal came together. He saw this as an opportunity for us to work together, satisfy some of his wanderlust, and to put another notch of success on his belt. He would work from home, travel to North Carolina once or twice a month, and call on potential customers, mostly in the Midwest and Southeast, as needed.

After getting Cecil to sign off, we needed to present the plan to the bank. The meeting with them was held in the conference room at our headquarters. In attendance representing the bank were Jonathon Gettys, one of Gettys' assistants, and Wynn Stroud. From our team, in addition to me, there were Cecil, Rick (whose hiring was pending the approval of the loan), Jerry Spade, Kirk, and Buddy. The presentation was to be an update of the plant's progress, and we were tacking on the loan request. The bank had been receiving monthly financial statements that showed we were now profitable, but I wasn't certain that they could forgive the past quite yet.

I was feeling pretty cocky going into the meeting. With an unnecessarily audacious attitude, I wore an old tie that I had received as a gag-gift one birthday. It had a picture of the Three Stooges from its top to bottom.

This was my back-handed tribute to our three visitors from Charlotte. I don't think they ever got it. If they did, no one commented. In the end, Thursby Plastics not only received their praise, we also got the money. And we went forward with the purchase, which turned out to be moderately successful but not the home run I had hoped for. After a year, the startup was finished, and we were in full production mode. Rick left the company to go back to his puttering, which he is still doing today.

# A Time to Spike the Ball

The big highlight moment came in the spring of 1994 after the 1993 results had been audited. Thursby Plastics had turned a profit at both plants. It was not a huge amount at the North Carolina plant, but it was significant enough to accept as a sign of future stability. We called all plant and headquarters personnel on first-shift to meet in the courtyard. I wanted Cecil to have the honor of making the announcement, and he readily accepted the invitation. After all, Cecil was responsible for having founded the business and all of its early success. I was merely there to put out a fire. Cecil proudly announced that profit-sharing was back and that everyone would receive a bonus of 3% of their pay each quarter of the current year as long as the company remained profitable.

People were stunned. They realized that they had been part of an almost miraculous turnaround and were now going to be rewarded. Very few were concerned that the amount was relatively small; it was the victory that mattered. We had the checks for the first quarter ready, and the managers and supervisors handed them out immediately. We asked Cecil to personally take care of giving checks to long-term employees. Most realized that their jobs were more secure than they had been for years. The payoff of many **MACHETE MOMENTS.**

There was a bi-product of this victory. The next morning, I was able to call the plant manager in Indiana with the news. I turned him loose to announce profit-sharing to his work force. They had heard about profit-sharing when they were hired, but because it was granted on company-wide, rather than plant results, they had almost given up hope of ever receiving it.

That evening, Cecil and I produced another shocker. We invited the management team and their wives to dinner in a private dining room at the Hotel Americaine.

It was first rate. There were shrimp cocktails, filet mignon, and exotic desserts. After the meal, I spoke in celebration of our accomplishments and turned the meeting over to Cecil. Not one to be great at publicly thanking people, he made brief comments that were heartfelt if less than effusive. That was forgotten once he got to the point. He passed out envelopes containing bonus checks totaling $100,000 among the nine recipients. I got $25,000 and the other eight split the remaining $75,000 with individual amounts ranging from $8,000 to $12,000.

The guys were ecstatic, and their wives were even more so. Cecil had always kept a tight hold on the purse strings and had never been one to reward only a few people for success. He much preferred giving 3% to everyone, as in the profit-sharing model. I had convinced him that this management team had gone through hell to save his company. They (we) deserved an additional reward. Further, this should be a precedent for future years. Most people work hard, but these were the leaders upon whom success depended. More pay off of **MACHETE MOMENTS.**

# Running a Family Business When You Are Not Family

Cecil and Elvina were proud of the fact that they never owned a television except one they bought a couple years earlier to watch educational, historical, and technical videos. It had never been connected to an antenna or cable. Cecil once told me that their six kids had never been exposed to such immoral nonsense. Of course, I heard from others that the kids went to the neighbors' every day to watch TV, but they never told their parents. Cecil had enjoyed two movies in his entire life, *A Chump at Oxford* with Laurel and Hardy and *Back to School* with Rodney Dangerfield. Go figure. Other than those exceptions, he never went to the movies or watched them on video. Instead, he dismissed all others out of hand as worthless crap.

The company kept two vehicles—a car and a van—on site in North Carolina to be used as needed by sales reps, engineers, and sometimes visitors. It was convenient to have them available. They saved wear and tear on personal vehicles, and they saved the cost of rentals. I wasn't sure the practice was economical, but it served a purpose. Elvina was afraid to drive the van; it was too big. Occasionally, she would use the car to run errands or pick someone up at the airport. And their grown children would often use them when they were in town—not quite within IRS regulations for a company vehicle but not a capital crime either. I decided to stay out of that one.

The Thursbys lived in an old farm house in a rural area of western North Carolina. On the few visits I made to their home, I saw a variety of dogs, cats, chickens, goats, and a llama. As nearly as I could tell, none of the animals seemed to serve a purpose. I never saw any evidence of loving them, as you might a pet, or of gathering eggs or milking the goats or whatever one does with a llama.

There was more than one occasion when an employee would go to use a vehicle for legitimate business only to find goat hair and other animal remnants in the back seat. It turned out that Elvina had occasionally borrowed the car to take one of the animals to the veterinarian. She said she did not want to mess up the back of their personal car or pickup truck. I decided that I had bigger issues to deal with, so I would not involve myself in that one either. They could do what they wanted with the assets of the business. They owned the company, and, by extension, they owned the vehicles. But it was a little embarrassing for a salesman to prepare to take customers to lunch only to be subjected to a back seat full of animal debris.

On three occasions, the Thursbys asked me to hire one of Jackie's friends who could not find work elsewhere. Usually, these guys had floated through multiple jobs in a short time and had run out of options. They had a couple of characteristics in common. They were all intelligent, but they all seemed to lack a rapport with mainstream society. The first, Cedric Brown, arrived at my doorstep just a few weeks after I started.

Ced had been a child of privilege, which may have accounted for his lack of a sense of urgency to succeed on his own. He and I hit it off at first because of our mutual love of variety of music genres, especially bluegrass. He claimed to have gone on a personal mission to track down bluegrass pioneer Ralph Stanley in the hills of Appalachia. As Ced tells it, they spent an afternoon on Ralph's front porch talking philosophy, drinking Jack Daniels, and picking guitars. Just before he came to Thursby, Ced was part of a failed new age music quartet—a viola, a concertina, a zither, and a tuba. Can't imagine why they didn't make it big.

I never did find out what Ced's degree was despite asking on many occasions. To avoid the perception of nepotism on the part of the Thursbys, Ced was assigned to me as a direct report. I gave him a job as liaison between the IT department and the rest of the organization. I asked Sally Cairo, who was serving as interim IT manager, to put up with him, and just keep him out of trouble. If she could find a way to make him productive, that would be whipped cream on the strawberries. Ced was with Thursby for about ten months and was often seen wandering around the office and the factory, but I never talked with anyone who knew of him actually doing any work. He left on his own as suddenly as he had arrived. I don't know where he went.

A couple of Jackie's other friends followed. They were decent enough people, albeit somewhat flaky, but none really fit into our organization. All of them departed within a year of hiring, and in the end probably did no harm. I thought maybe they could have become doctors having already fulfilled the first requirement in the Hippocratic Oath.

# Time to Manage a Personal Crisis

All three of my hand-picked hires in 1993-94 fit perfectly onto the barstools at Nat's and were a great comfort to me in my life on the road. While Rick and Bill were in town only sporadically, I had at least one of three with me enough to ease the loneliness. Sometimes the beers made my mouth move a little too much. Late one night when all four of us were at Nat's, I shared the story of Jeff's conception. It was the day Kate and I moved to Vienna. We were in our new apartment because we couldn't afford a hotel. The furniture had not yet arrived. One thing led to another, and the conception took place on the floor after our two children were tucked into sleeping bags in what would become their bedroom. I think that was more than Jeff wanted to know. But it's one of those things that, once said, you can't take back.

As the months turned to years, the shallowness of having a bar as my only outlet for stress crept into my conscious mind, and whatever joy life at Nat's had brought me, turned to depression. I was getting home for one three-day weekend a month, and each quarter, I stayed home for a ten-day stretch. But it wasn't enough. All of the facets of turnaround management had gotten to me. Every time I had to fire someone, I suffered. I realized that each of my victims suffered more, but the guilt and second-guessing piled up. Hadn't there been an alternative? The truth was that if I hadn't done it, someone else would have been hired to do it, or the company would have gone broke. Except for Dan and Carroll, I was haunted by the memory of everyone who was out of work because I had a job to do. I'm sure the drinking didn't help either.

Spending time with Jeff, Rick, and Bill meant a lot, but there was too much time that they weren't there. One important benefit was that the situation gave me the opportunity to become closer friends with my son than I ever would have otherwise. However, when I was alone, I sank back into melancholia. I was depressed and having serious suicidal thoughts. I was confused, and every time I thought through my feelings, I ended up with the conclusion that I didn't want to live anymore. I really believe that, if I had been the only one affected, I would have pulled the trigger. However, I had read enough about the effect that suicide would have on my family, who truly loved me, that I backed off.

# Another Beginning of Another End

The rotten cherry on my sour sundae came in August 1994. I was more than three years into this routine. I had pretty much forgotten what a normal life looked like. Cecil came to me one day and wanted to have a management getaway at a ski resort about ninety minutes north of Harper. In the warm months, the place courted groups to have conferences on their site to help them cover their costs until their busy season. I was quite surprised that the idea of a retreat came from Cecil. He had made the point many times as to how he did not enjoy meetings.

On the surface, the retreat seemed to be a good idea, and I asked Bill Rocco to proceed to make arrangements. Cecil and I and the eight person management team would travel on Wednesday morning in the company vehicles. We would get there for lunch and have a meeting in the afternoon. Although Jackie was technically not part of the management team, Cecil wanted him to be there. He would be coming from a different direction and would drive separately. Cecil told me that he would like to say a few words after dinner. The group would return home Thursday afternoon after meetings and lunch.

For the agenda on Wednesday afternoon, three or four people were assigned to make presentations to the group to familiarize the others about their respective functions. Then they were to facilitate a discussion as to how they might work together with the other areas for the betterment of the organization. There was nothing remarkable about the presentations, but coupled with the discussions, they seemed somewhat valuable. The group adjourned to a pretty good buffet dinner.

Then it came time for Cecil to address the assembled masses. He spoke for about twenty minutes using some of his regular stories and a reiteration of the concern he had for the well-being of his employees. Then he proceeded to announce that he was thinking about retiring "before long". He gave no indication of a time frame for that action. That was followed by the surprising news that he would be succeeded as CEO by his son Jackie. He continued by extolling Jackie's virtues and expressing how proud he was of the way Jackie had grown to a point that he was comfortable leaving him in charge of the business. There was no mention of my future position with the company, but it was clear that I would not be the next CEO. As I said earlier, I went into this job with my eyes open about how minds can change in a family business. That didn't lessen my hurt and disappointment.

I left the dining room immediately after Cecil's talk, declining invitations to stay for a last drink. I couldn't sleep. I got up about 1 AM, packed my duffel bag, and headed back to Harper in the van. It was my intention to drive it to the airport the next morning, call Bill Rocco to tell him where he could pick up the vehicle, and get on the first plane out of town. As I approached Harper, good sense overruled my anger. I remembered that we had a daughter that we still had to educate. It was no time to be out of a job, and leaving in such a manner would certainly diminish my value and credibility on the job market.

I made a U-turn and got back to the hotel about four AM. As far as I knew, no one ever knew that I had been gone, except that I did tell Bill Rocco at breakfast what I had done. Bill said that he had looked for me after dinner because he knew what I was feeling. He then promised to talk to Cecil, which he did before the morning's meeting began. Cecil then tried to explain his decision to me, but I only half listened. It just didn't matter. I appreciated the attempt, but it didn't make up for my disheartenment. When I returned to Indiana, I immediately started preparations for a job search. I no longer felt any obligation to Thursby Plastics.

I went through the motions of being COO for another three months while cutting back on the frequency and duration of my trips to North Carolina. Finally, in early December, Cecil told me that he was promoting Jackie to COO and that he wanted me to go back and continue to be in charge of the Indiana operation. I knew there was no job there for me there. I had replaced myself in Indiana with a general manager who had all manufacturing and sales functions reporting to him. He was doing a fine job, and I was not going to get rid of him to find a spot for myself. So I went home and intensified my search.

In the months between the debacle on the mountain and December, Elvina visited me a couple of times in my North Carolina office. She seemed to be aware of the impact the announcement had on me. I told her that I wasn't going to be around forever and that the company needed to ensure that they were able to cover whatever I had brought to the party. She was obviously aware that I was hurt by the change of direction. She confirmed what I already realized. Cecil was determined to keep the business in the family. In one of the visits to my office, she asked that if I left, what I thought would be a fair reward in the form of severance for what I had done for the company and the family. I had to do some quick thinking. If I told her what I really thought they owed me, I risked creating sticker shock and getting nothing. I told her that I would be satisfied with a year's pay and full family benefits for that time.

I went back to headquarters in February for a meeting with the bankers, but that would be my last trip to North Carolina as an employee of Thursby Plastics. I spent the first four months of 1995 in my Indiana office doing pretty much nothing related to the company. Most of my time was focused on looking for a job. In early May, Cecil and Elvina visited me for a meeting of just the three of us. We all agreed that my time with the company should end. I got the year of full salary and benefits and an agreement that I could keep my office as a place from which to conduct a job search. I did not receive the bonus I had gotten the past two years, but I decided not to make a big deal of that. I took what I had and got out. I was relieved and happy to be gone. What do you know? I had been there seven years almost to the day.

Coincidentally, the general manager, whom I had refused to replace with myself, had resigned to take a better job two weeks before my meeting with the Thursbys. By then, I was too far along in my bitterness and desire to move on. I never considered moving into that job again. I had to leave. When it was clear that I was leaving, I recommended to Cecil that he promote Bill Muldoon, who was still sales manager, to be general manager of Indiana operations. Cecil thought that was a good idea and followed through. In about a year, Jackie told Bill that he wanted to build his own team. Bill, who was already fielding job-offers from other companies, received what he later told me was a fair severance package and left quietly. In another six years, the Indiana business was sold to a plastics manufacturer from the south and is still in operation today.

# Looking Back from the Present

There were actually several happy endings to my experiences at Thursby. In 2008, Jackie sold the company to Bannion Industries, a large plastics manufacturer with an international market that was looking to add rotational molding to its stable of processes. They kept the company whole, for the most part, including maintaining the management team and the location south of Harper. The plant has been expanded, and sales have grown beyond anyone's expectations.

Many of the managers that I put in place are still there. Cecil and Jerry Spade have retired. Ted Danvers, Kirk Gillis, and Buddy Strasser are secure in their jobs. Bill Rocco left a couple of years ago to take a job as human resources director with a larger company in Greensboro. I had hired an IT manager when I was there who came and went in two years. Toward the end of my time, I told Sally Cairo that she was ready for the job without the interim tag. I have heard that she has done and is still doing an outstanding job. Jackie is not associated with the company except as a stockholder.

As for my son, Jeff, he thrived after the sale of the company and is now in a management role for a division of Bannion Industries. He considers himself fortunate in that Bannion is a first-rate organization that holds to the same high moral and ethical standards as Cecil Thursby instilled in his company many decades ago. Jeff's office remains at the former Thursby facility in North Carolina. He married a young woman from the area, and they still live there happily with their three sons. Jeff and his family are one of many parts of my family that give me a reason to be proud.

A combination of good people at all levels and quality products has enabled Thursby Plastics to remain profitable without me. And the purchase of the company by Bannion Industries several years ago infused some new talent that enhanced that success. I am sincerely happy that everything turned out well for my former associates. It gives me a warm feeling that I might have had something to do with laying the foundation for that success.

Going back to an observation made a decade earlier, I agree that I am a pretty good dragon-slayer, but I believe others are better equipped to run an ongoing manufacturing operation. I think the difference is that the turnarounds I stepped into had solutions that were people based. Once a plant or a company is operating efficiently, more technical skills are needed. I guess we all have our specialties.

# V.

# THE DECISION AND PROCESS OF MAKING A DRASTIC CAREER CHANGE

As I mentioned in the Burnout section, I was sitting on an offer to become vice-president of operations for a Japanese-owned company located in Vienna. Because it was another turnaround, I was dragging my feet. Deep down, I knew that I didn't have the fire in my belly to go through that again. One positive characteristic I had always possessed was the ability to get up for a big challenge. That was not the case now. I believed I was certain to fail.

On the other hand, those recruiting me for the United Way job emphasized the need for a turnaround in that organization. The annual fund raising campaign had stagnated from years of weak leadership and from a scandal three years earlier when the president of the national organization had been caught with his fingers in the till. That never sets well with contributors to a charity.

It's strange that while the manufacturing turnaround scared me, the need for a turnaround at United Way was an exciting possibility. I think the difference was that the manufacturing challenge was just too similar to my Thursby experience. On the other hand, the United Way task would be a whole new adventure. There was another compelling factor that tipped the scale to United Way. I was told that the non-profit sector did not "have a seat at the table" in our community. Vienna and Sierra County have many initiatives for which local leaders from the business, government, and education sectors gather to discuss various subjects related to local quality of life and to develop plans for improvement. Successful results of such activities are essential, especially to the big companies in the area that recruit from the Ivy League, Stanford, Duke, Notre Dame, and other schools of similar stature. Those companies know very well that their recruits have many choices. In order to be competitive in acquiring their share of the top talent, Sierra County has to be an attractive option.

Over the years, there have been scores of task forces, committees, focus groups, panels, and about any other handle you can put on people coming together for a specific purpose. Some of the issues have been the development of a community 10-year strategic plan, making the community welcoming to a diverse mix of people, revitalization of the downtown, expanding the arts and other cultural resources, economic development with an emphasis on recruiting foreign-based companies, and more. There you have the foundation of why Vienna is often referred to as a quintessential community. Many important issues are addressed by a cross-section of leaders, and yet, in 1995 no one was invited to represent the human services sector.

I took the job as president of the Sierra County United Way on the condition that I would be there for two years to lead the turnaround. Then, I would turn it over to a non-profit professional and go back to the manufacturing world where I belonged. Within a few weeks, I must have heard a dozen people comment about how much more relaxed I seemed to be and how they had been worried about me as I showed the strain of my former job. The time to return to manufacturing never came. In the mornings, I was never tempted to crawl back between the sheets. Every evening as I drove home, I felt that I had done something worthwhile. In short, I had found contentment. My manufacturing career was over just like that. A huge **MACHETE MOMENT.**

# VI.

# A REBIRTH–THE NON-PROFIT YEARS

## Another Rookie Year

In August 1995, a new day dawned on my life. I began what would become a seventeen year term as president of United Way of Sierra County in our hometown of Vienna, Indiana. I could not have landed in a more fertile field for raising money and recruiting volunteers. Sierra County was unusual for a community of 70,000 in that it was the location of the corporate headquarters of not one, but two, Fortune 500 companies, Denard, Inc. and Munsey Industries. Combining corporate contributions and money received from internal employee campaigns, these two organizations were responsible for about half of the $1.4 million United Way had garnered the year before I arrived. Even with that advantage, we lagged behind several other United Ways in the state in per capita giving.

The presence of the corporate headquarters of those two companies meant that there were a disproportionate number of high-paying jobs including several seven-digit ones. Given the culture created by the many philanthropists in town and reinforced by the community minded principles ingrained in Denard, Munsey, and the Lime-Desmond Foundation, you could not stand on a downtown street corner and swing a dead cat without hitting three or four do-gooders.

My first day on the job, I deliberately arrived about an hour after starting time so that I could meet the staff as a group, rather than one at a time. The staff was composed of four women. There was a campaign director who coordinated the raising of money through an annual campaign. The allocations director supported the volunteers on the citizens review committee. This group studied agency funding applications for the following year's allocations, met with agency leaders, and recommended to the board how much money each agency would receive. There were also a secretary and the director of First Call for Help.

First Call was functionally separate from United Way but had been put under the same roof several years earlier. It is a resource and referral source that people can access to learn where to find the resources to address their particular needs. First Call was downstairs in the same building as United Way. I just assumed that it was in my purview, and the director never pushed back. That organization has now become part of national service called 211, but it retains its local office and is still a division of United Way. Just as you can call 911 to report an emergency, or call 411 to get telephone numbers, you can call 211 and be connected to your nearest resource and referral agency. Our 211 organization has expanded to serve several southern Indiana counties in addition to Sierra.

When I started in August, the 1995 annual fund-raising campaign team was already in place and moving forward. The campaign in Sierra County runs approximately from Labor Day to Thanksgiving, but the assignments to volunteers who solicit contributions are made earlier.

I wanted to meet with as many of the community's movers and shakers as possible in order to give each of them the opportunity to tell me what they expected of United Way and me. I made about forty such visits. The folks I visited really seemed to appreciate my interest in their expectations, and many seemed surprised to be asked. I got the impression that none of my predecessors over many years had bothered to ask the opinions of our community leaders.

Because my meetings occurred in the fall, I combined those visits with requests for personal, corporate, and employee contributions to the campaign. Many of the answers were of the nature that it was too late to make a difference for this year. I heard of budgets already having been determined with no increases in charitable giving. Another frequent reply was that it was too late to fit an employee campaign into their schedules. I saw these as unwinnable battles and decided not to push very hard.

Instead, I preferred to get a commitment to work with me early the next year to get United Way into their budgets and schedules.

By the next March, I got back to everyone I had visited to discuss in more depth about what giving to United Way meant to the community and how I expected them to help. Rather than taking a posture of begging, I chose share my opinion that participation is part of the price of doing business in our community. My charge to CEO's and HR directors I met with was that giving individually and as a company was their responsibility as business leaders. The second part of my assignment to them was that they should enable their employees to give by conducting a high-profile internal campaign. I made a pretty big deal of how we had implemented many of the suggestions they had made in our first conversation. That was fairly easy because, just as at Thursby Plastics five years earlier, the suggestions overlapped so that I could boil them down to four or five without losing their identity. To a person, they seemed to be impressed that I had listened and had acted so quickly. In seven months, I had established credibility with the town's most influential leaders. In fact, I had already earned my "seat at the table" and was beginning to be invited to represent the non-profit sector in community planning activities.

For the most part, I would describe the reaction of the United Way staff, the leaders of the agencies, and other volunteers who showed up at various meetings around the community, as intimidated. I was a big guy who said exactly what I thought and expected others to do the same. I spoke softly but firmly and used humor when it was appropriate and sometimes when it wasn't. I never deliberately embarrassed anyone, having been a victim of that tactic early in my career. But I did swear, which I toned down in later years. Yet, I'm sure that many of my new associates saw me as a fire-breathing dragon. All but one of the office staff I inherited quit within a year, and that was all right with me. I was able to put together my own team.

To about a dozen of my colleagues, I was what they had been waiting for. They saw the potential in what they perceived as strong leadership. Together, we made up a critical mass that could drive success. Vienna is a manufacturing town, and as an alumnus of the manufacturing fraternity, I had access to all of those business leaders. The other human service agency leaders that had bought into my leadership believed me when I said United

Way could conduct a two-million dollar campaign without increasing expenses. That would allow us to pass the entire increase (almost a half-million dollars) through to the funding of agencies.

The campaign that had begun when I arrived, closed at about $1.5 million, a 6% increase over the prior year. I took no credit for that result. I think the die was cast before I started. My contribution was that I had planted a whole garden full of seeds that could be harvested the next campaign and beyond.

# My Coming-Out Party

Six months after my start date, I continued a tradition that called for United Way to host its Annual Meeting every February. The event is usually attended by 200-300 residents. There are corporate, government, and non-profit leaders, media, and other community minded citizens. Over the years, it took various forms—a breakfast, a lunch, and a late afternoon gathering with a cocktail hour afterward. At my first Annual Meeting, a luncheon, I initiated a custom that would remain for the seventeen years I would be president. I gave a State of the United Way address. The one constant in those seventeen speeches was that I always talked briefly about campaign results. I also tried to present a challenge that the community needed to address as a priority. These challenges took the form of identifying specific problems and opportunities. I shared plans for future initiatives that United Way should either lead or participate in under the leadership of others. Some of the more noteworthy ones I wanted us to take the lead on were early child development (including child care), domestic violence awareness and prevention, and volunteerism.

I became recognized and respected as the expert on subjects related to human services in the community. I'm not sure that perception was true, but I accepted the responsibility that goes with that reputation.

At that first Annual Meeting, I placed a can of dog food on each table with no upfront explanation. During the address, I made the point that we spent more on dog food in our county than we contributed to United Way and that we needed to reconsider our priorities. I assured the dog lovers that I didn't want to starve their dogs, but I thought that humans who were in need deserved at least equal attention. In the post-meeting schmoozing,

I heard many positive reactions regarding both the analogy and the general upbeat and informative tone of the talk. I heard no complaints from dog lovers.

# Two important new relationships

One of my new colleagues was Shirley Blaine, the program director of Lime-Desmond Foundation. LDF was a large family foundation that for decades had made major contributions in support of worthy organizations and initiatives. Shirley and I had many conversations about the wrongs in the world and our wishes for what could be. Many of those wishes soon turned into plans. And the plans were followed by actions. Possibly the best part of our relationship was that Shirley had the balls to tell me when she thought I was wrong. I soon learned that she was not a chronic naysayer and that when she disagreed, I should pay attention. It was an invaluable partnership.

Shirley was a relief from the many colleagues who always deferred to me because of the perceived importance of my position. I never knew what those people really thought. Given their apprehensive manner, I could never trust them completely as team mates. The willingness to disagree with the boss is an undervalued and uncommon characteristic. I think that so many people are afraid of losing their jobs, that they accept whatever crap their leader hands out. A leader who reprimands subordinates when they state an honest disagreement is not much of a leader. She doesn't get the full value out of employees. Conversely, employees who won't speak up when they have a disagreement with their boss are not fulfilling their potential. Shirley had bigger balls than any of the men I encountered in my early days in the human services industry.

Another partnership I developed was with the president of our community foundation. Within two years, I was invited to fill a seat on its board. She and I had an informal agreement that United Way would take care of human services, and the community foundation would deal with the arts, business development, education, and infrastructure. We often worked together on overarching issues. She and I had many discussions about opportunities and problems that were of mutual interest.

In general, people give to United Way from income and give to the community foundation endowments from wealth. In Sierra County, the two organizations never fought over money. We both encouraged those with greater than average means not to choose, but to give to both. A couple of years ago, I was at a meeting with about a dozen presidents of the larger United Ways around the state. One agenda item was a discussion of each United Way's relationship with the community foundation in its county. I listened as half of the group told their stories. The relationships were described as tolerant or adversarial or aloof or friendly but never as close. They were surprised when I testified that our community fund and United Way collaborate on many community issues and that, in fact, I was a member of its board.

## This Could Be the Start of Something Big

My second year was even more eventful than the first. I recruited the president of the community's largest bank as our volunteer campaign chair. He was a jovial, generous man who was well thought of in the community. We decided to take a moon shot and set a goal of two-million dollars for the fall campaign. It surprised many that we jacked up the target so quickly. That meant that success would require an increase of more than 30%. We didn't make it, but there was evidence that the seeds were growing. We closed half of the gap coming in at $1,750,000—a 17% increase over the previous year.

Although we had fallen short of the goal, everyone felt good that we were able to break our record aggregate allocations to agencies by over a quarter-million dollars. And in the same press release in which the campaign total was announced, we set the following year's goal at that same two million bucks.

On the personal side, I had both knees replaced in November 1996. Everyone who had an opinion said that, at 55, I was too young to go to such an extreme. But the pain was ruining all the good things in my life. Every step was excruciating and had been for several years. My Dad had had the same problem, so I just thought it was a natural part of the aging process. In the late eighties, I virtually had to give up tennis, which I love, and take up golf, which I don't love. I had to play from a cart, and it still hurt because I had to walk around the tees and greens. I'm sure the pain contributed to the depression I experienced at Thursby. In those years, it hurt not only to walk around the plant, but the 230 yard walk to and from Nat's was almost more than I could bear. Here's a tip to those readers who share this ailment. Don't hesitate to take the plunge to a joint replacement if you are in pain. As I said in the beginning of the book, this was one of the three best decisions I ever made.

Anuja Renault was president of the Lime-Desmond Foundation. She had moved from India to Vienna in the sixties with her family and had become quite Americanized while still holding to the values and traditions of her birthplace. Her husband had been an engineer at Denard. He had been killed in a plane crash in 1975. Anuja had worked her way up through the ranks at Lime-Desmond and was a hard-driving, brilliant strategic thinker. She married a university professor from France in the eighties and has led a happy and successful life since. She can be described as the epitome of a really good person—caring of others, considerate, and selfless.

All of her qualities made her the perfect candidate to serve as volunteer chair of the campaign. It was imperative that we reach the two-million dollar goal this time, lest the community start to lose confidence in me. Part of the job of campaign chair is to work with the campaign director on our staff and me in recruiting division chairs. These are the people who solicit contributions from organizations in various segments of the community. There are divisions for manufacturing, government, retail, education, and so on. The selection is a delicate task because you want people with name recognition so that their target audience will take their calls. But often the schedules of leaders of that strength are so crowded that they don't get around to making the calls. In that event, the staff ends up doing the work late in the campaign.

Anuja is a woman to whom it is extremely hard to say no. If you try, she will ask why and then explain to you what you have to do to say yes. Through it all, she is frighteningly polite so that if you finally say no, you will feel guilty for the rest of your life. In most campaigns, you end up with division chairs that are good people but are second or third level managers and supervisors in their respective organizations.

But Anuja chose not to settle for less than the best. She recruited two bank presidents, a general manager at a large chain store, a couple of successful business owners, and other high caliber leaders as division chairs. Her real coup was gaining the agreement of Ted Leland, the CEO of Denard, Inc., to lead the individual donors division. This division is comprised of people who would not be reached in an employee campaign because they are either retired or are entrepreneurs and professionals who operate their own one- or two-person businesses. There are many deep pockets scattered through this population.

Ted had been recruited by Denard out of college and was identified early as top management material. The company had moved him methodically through all the right chairs, assigning him to manage a plant, direct human relations, and manage marketing of its largest business segment. At forty-six, he was appointed president and two years later was promoted to chairman/CEO. As luck would have it, he no sooner got the job that the market went to hell. Denard sales and profits went with it.

The price of Denard stock was lower than it had been for decades. Downsizing in every area of the business was brutal. Executive bonuses were eliminated, as were scholarships for the children of employees. Ted sold junk bonds to infuse cash into the operation.

He took two years of shots across the bow from Wall Street analysts, who demanded that he participate in a weekly conference call with them. He was also severely criticized by the analysts for adhering to Denard's policy of community service and philanthropy. Most of these hot-shots were twenty-eight years old, but they knew everything— everything except an understanding of altruism and compassion.

New government imposed regulations threatened to bring production to a halt. Rumors were rampant about the possibility of Denard being purchased by a larger company. If that happened, surely the headquarters would be moved out.

Two years earlier, Munsey had merged with Ugarte Manufacturing, which was headquartered in Minnesota, and had moved their higher ranking people there. The departure of Denard would have meant that Sierra County had lost the headquarters of two Fortune 500 companies in three years. Such a blow would have killed the local economy. The domino effect would have ruined many local retailers, service businesses, and others that counted on the revenue generated by Denard, Munsey, and their employees.

Instead of folding his tent, Ted chose to be aggressive. While competitors were fighting with Congress to get the standards softened, Ted declared that Denard was going to meet the standards. The Wall Street gang was impressed by his extreme actions. Within two years, the company had met the standards, which eventually led to record sales and profits. Denard's success in meeting the standards caused its competitors to lose their fight with the government. That created a competitive advantage from which the others have still not recovered.

Normally, the campaign cabinet met two or three times over the course of the campaign, and attendance was far from 100%. Anuja hosted a cabinet meeting *every* Tuesday at 7 AM for three months in the basement conference room of the Lime-Desmond building. She required division chairs to account for their division's progress in the past week. At the first meeting, she introduced a brick that would be the symbol of failure each week. The division chair with the least progress had to carry the brick until the next week's meeting. One week there were two people who could report no progress. Anuja brought out a second brick she had been holding in reserve for such an eventuality.

Denard's corporate office building is about six blocks from the Lime-Desmond building. One cold early-November Tuesday morning, I parked on the street in front of the building a little before 7. About a block away, here came Ted Leland walking down the street carrying the brick. I joked about being out so early. Ted said he was afraid to miss the meeting because, "Anuja would make me carry this Goddamn brick for another week." Here was the CEO of one of the top corporations in the nation, and he was wary of Anuja's wrath.

The woman had no fear. She did everything first rate and expected others to do the same. Fifteen years of political correctness and coddling our kids since that campaign have driven us away from such negative reinforcement techniques, but I'll tell you, they weren't all that bad. The brick was done good-naturedly, but it made its point. Now we've raised a whole generation that has been so buffered from criticism that they would burst into tears if you gave them a brick. Today, they all expect a trophy for just showing up.

As you may have guessed by now, we made the goal. However, in the end we had to take one special action. The day before we were to announce the total, we were $24,000 short and had made every call we could think of to beg for more. A stroke of good fortune was the fact that the Lime-Desmond Management Company, the parent of the foundation, owned the building that housed the United Way offices. For years, it had quietly donated the space. Since no money changed hands, there had been no recognition in the United Way campaign results. At the last minute, Anuja realized this oversight and decided that United Way should recognize the contribution of the building as a gift-in-kind. She set the rent at $2,000 a month or $24,000 annually. We recorded it as a gift-in-kind and made the goal. It was all legitimate and something we should have done all along, but neither I nor anyone else had ever thought about it.

The following year, the goal was set at $2.1 million, and we made it. United Way of Sierra County has never again slipped below two million dollars. What had been thought of as impossible had become routine. As with most things considered routine, it took a lot of hard work and innovative thinking by staff and volunteers to make it appear that way, but we never again had to resort to creative accounting.

Ted and I became great friends during and after that campaign. He once introduced me to a group of people at a gathering. In telling the audience what he liked about me, Ted declared, "He moves the furniture." I took that as a compliment and treasure that metaphor to this day. Nike has it right with their "Just Do It" slogan. I can't understand why we have to make life so difficult when most tasks can be so simple.

# Shake it up, baby

In the early part of the new millennium, the campaign had become stuck between 2 and 2.2 million dollars for five years. It was generating new and increased contributions, but those were being offset by Munsey's ever-decreasing local employment and several closings of small businesses.

At that time, Denard's combined corporate and employee giving accounted for about 35% of the total campaign income. The company donated $400,000; the employee campaign generated another $300,000. The company's sales and profits had been down since 1997. Along with that, management bonuses were all but non-existent. It didn't help that there was a recession in 2001. Those may have been reasons for stagnation, but they were no longer acceptable as excuses. It had been too long since United Way had had a dramatic increase in funds raised.

At the 2001 Annual Meeting, I stood in front of about 300 business, government, and non-profit agency leaders and announced record campaign results. Then I scolded them. I claimed that we should be raising the equivalent of a buck a week or $50 for every person in the county. With a population of 70,000, the arithmetic said that our campaign should raise $3,500,000. I thought it was unreasonable to expect those with low incomes to give more than a token amount. That left it to those of us with jobs providing median income or more and the profitable businesses with the responsibility for providing the increase.

Most contributors to our United Way campaign give with no strings. That money is made available to our citizens review committee for their study and recommendation. Rather than make a contribution to the general campaign, about 30% of the donors choose to designate their gifts to an agency of their choice. The designee may or may not be one of our certified agencies. It can be any non-profit organization in the country except governments, schools, and faith-based organizations.

Beginning in 2004, Denard began a dramatic and sustained return to profitability, but its total employee contributions to United Way did not increase. In looking for a root cause, I discovered that a couple of years earlier, Ted Leland had issued an edict that employees could not designate their contributions to the Boy Scouts. Ted was an avid advocate of non-discrimination. Equality and diversity had been cornerstones of Denard policy since its founding. Managers who disregarded that policy didn't rise within the company. When Boy Scouts stated its policy barring homosexuals from leadership roles, Ted acted. He was not going to support that organization in any way. That resolve included a refusal for the company to serve as a pass-through agent for designated donations. The conservative portion of the work force reacted as might be expected. Many refused to contribute to United Way. As is often the case with large work places, the attitude spread like wildfire, even with those who couldn't have cared less about Ted's position regarding the Boy Scouts. They were pissed off at being told to whom they could and couldn't give.

I went to Ted and told him of the collateral damage he was causing. He was torn between his principles and the idea of costing the needy of our county potentially hundreds of thousands of dollars annually in services. I needed to find a face-saving way out for Ted. Finally, I offered to inform the Boy Scouts' top management that, while Denard would honor employees' wishes and collect designated donations to Boy Scouts through payroll deductions, not one dollar of the corporate contribution would go to Boy Scouts. This is what is called a negative designation. It really doesn't change the amount an organization receives in total, but it sends a message that the CEO of a major donor strongly objects to the Boy Scouts' policy. Ted agreed to the compromise. A **MACHETE MOMENT** to build on.

While I was on a roll, I decided to push a little further. I told Ted that I thought his decision would create conditions whereby the employee campaign might grow to what had previously been an unthinkable amount. I asked him to commit to a dollar-for-dollar company match of employee giving. We adjourned without Ted having answered that request.

I credit my friend on the inside, Trish Murdock, director of community responsibility at Denard and president of the Denard Foundation. She had become a valued colleague and friend. We worked together on everything tied to the United Way-Denard relationship. Trish set up meetings with Ted and ran interference for me on issues we wanted to discuss with him. She was a great partner to work with throughout my entire career at United Way. I'm sure that she made comments to Ted in support of my request.

About two weeks after I had met with Ted, Trish called with the news that I was invited to attend Ted's monthly operating committee meeting. She was somewhat flabbergasted as she told me that no one not involved directly in Denard business had ever been invited to this meeting. The operating committee consists of the CEO, the president, and ten vice-presidents. When one refers to top management, these are the people he is talking about.

I was called into the meeting for discussion of a single topic. Actually, to call it a discussion is inaccurate. It was an edict. Apparently, without discussing it with any of his top aides, Ted announced his amended position on Boy Scouts designations *and* promised that the company would match employee giving 100%. Further, this commitment *would* receive top-down support. Success or failure would be part of the year-end evaluation of everyone in the room and their subordinate directors and managers. WOW!

His commitment was so strong that I felt compelled to get a potential problem on the table. I warned, "Wait a minute, Ted. What if the employee campaign grows to a million dollars?" Without hesitation, Ted said, "Then United Way will receive a check from the Denard Foundation for a million dollars." A **MACHETE MOMENT** piggy-backed onto another **MACHETE MOMENT.**

The next campaign raised $750,000 from Denard employees, which was matched by the company. In 2011, employee giving totaled $1.5 million. The company gave $1.5 million.

Beginning in 2003, the overall United Way campaign grew by about a quarter-million dollars a year. In 2007 my challenge of $3.5 million was achieved. Except for the recession period of 2008-2010, a record has been set every year culminating in the raising of $3.75 million in 2011. How ironic it was that Denard, the company whose pay scale caused one of my biggest problems at Kane, was now my most valuable resource and strongest supporter. The momentum continued without me. In 2012, the new kid in my old seat proved himself by producing our first four-million dollar campaign in his first year on the job.

As a footnote to the story, I made the challenge to the community and the subsequent visits to Ted entirely on my own. I did not run the ideas by the board of directors or anyone else. This was the modus operandi I had established when I arrived on the job and continued throughout my administration. This tactic of assumption of authority became noticeably unpopular with the board in my final three years. I had been urged to come to this job; I hadn't applied for it. I took that as implied authority to lead the board rather than have the board lead me. This concept was never spoken or written, but no one ever argued with it for the first fourteen years of my administration. More on that issue later.

# The Undertow of Dependency

So what does the human services industry do with all those millions raised by our United Way? The money is allocated to various non-profit organizations in Sierra County that provide services for people in need. For most of the people who require those services, the primary reason for their need is poverty. Whatever other problems they might have in their lives, poverty usually is a major driving force. The old axiom that money does not buy happiness is true, but the other side of that is that it is difficult to be very happy without it.

Since you are reading this book, it's probable that you take self-sufficiency somewhat for granted. You have a job that provides an income that is at least enough to fill your individual and your family's basic needs. It probably provides some level of health benefits and maybe even a 401-k with a company match. You have a home, which you either own or rent. You have a car for each adult in the household. And if needed, you can pay for quality child care.

However, there are thousands of people in our community that don't fit that description. Let's look at how two hypothetical women handle the situation. They are both single mothers, and we're going to give both of them two children, ages three and seven. The first works in a factory and makes the national average for that type of work, $19.17 an hour. Should she be able to live pretty well on that? We'll see. The second works in retail sales at the national average, $10.15 an hour. Can she make ends meet by cutting some corners?

Each lives in a two-bedroom apartment in a low-cost development. She has a used car that she financed at $150 a month, and she buys a 15-gallon tank of gas every other week. Her employer provides individual health insurance for its employees. However, she has to pay one-third of the additional cost to the employer for dependent coverage ($450 x 1/3 = $150). Her three-year-old goes to a licensed child care center every day. The seven-year-old goes there after school for half the full-time cost.

Since monthly numbers are easiest to relate to, I will use that format. National averages for expenses are a little hard to come by because they vary widely by location, but I will use the middle ground. We will assume a frugal lifestyle for both families.

## THE PLIGHT OF TWO MOMS

| | MOM 1 | MOM 2 |
|---|---|---|
| Income at 40 hours/week | $3,514 | $1,860 |
| Taxes withheld (Fed. & State) | 878 (25%) | 372 (20%) |
| Monthly take home pay | $2636 | $1,488 |
| Basic expenses: | | |
| Rent and utilities | $700 | $700 |
| Groceries | 500 | 500 |
| Transportation | 250 | 250 |
| Health insurance | 150 | 150 |
| Child Care | 900 | 900 |
| Total basic expenses | $2,500 | $2,500 |
| **Net cash flow** | **136** | **-1,112** |

Mom 1 has $136 a month left for clothing, school expenses (supplies, lunches, and field trips), medical co-pays, entertainment, and whatever else comes up. She might make it, but there is certainly no room for emergencies which inevitably happen when you have two children.

Mom 2 is just screwed. She could cancel her insurance and leave the kids home alone, and she still can't make it. On the assumption that Mom 1 is living frugally and only covering the basics, Mom 2's expenses will be no less. What does either Mom do on a day when her child care arrangements fall through? She can call in sick. In time, that will get her fired. It's unthinkable that she would leave the seven-year-old home to watch the three-year-old. That is totally unacceptable to the extent that child protective services would take the children away from her. And even if she magically finds free reliable, quality child care, Mom 2 is still $212 a month short of being able to pay for basic expenses.

Are there other alternatives? (1) Mom can quit her job, stay home with the kids, and go on welfare. (2) She can move back in with her parents or other relatives, neither of which welcome her and her children who are infringing on their lives. There is rarely room for two generations of adults to live under the same roof for very long, and the addition of a third generation doesn't usually improve things. (3) And the worst alternative— she can get into that chain of loveless relationships and move in with some guy so that there will be two incomes. I can't begin to list the negative outcomes that can come from that choice.

Once a person has a reason to enter "the system", it is next to impossible to get out. More often than not, people have more than one problem, and they all need to be solved or, at least, become manageable to reach an acceptable level of self-sufficiency.

Earlier I mentioned my stick drawings. Here is one that depicts a woman who has been in need of services and is trying to attain self-sufficiency. As she reaches for safety, an undertow keeps pulling her back. That undertow includes all of the barriers to self-sufficiency that might exist in her life. Every one of them has to be under control, or she will slip back into the need for assistance. If any one component gets out of control, she will become a victim of the undertow.

# THE UNDERTOW OF DEPENDENCY

SELF-SUFFICIENCY

Can't afford quality child care
Other problems with kids
No reliable transportation
Violence at home
Inadequate housing
Lack of education/training

It is difficult for members of non-profit boards to relate to the myriad problems of those who are dependent on the human services system. Board members usually come from lives of plenty. Most of them have never lived in dependency and are not close to anyone who has. They can sympathize, but they can't fully understand the complexity of the situation. A person of means knows that people in need can participate in a program to deal with domestic violence or one that provides assistance in paying for child care. What they tend not to understand is how every component in a client's particular bag of problems has to be at an acceptable level of control, or she is once again sucked into the undertow. The professionals who work in human services understand because they live with it every day. However, human services jobs tend to pay so little that many of those professionals are also clients of one or more agencies.

Herein lays the rub. The members of the board of directors, while charged with the well-being of the agency, often don't relate to the market. They can't possibly feel the need to the degree necessary for them to make the best decisions for those in need. This brings me to a good time to share my views on the CEO/Board relationship.

# The Nature of Non-profit Boards—Sometimes They Help, and Sometimes They Help More by Getting Out of the Way

My comments here reflect my observations of non-profit boards in general over seventeen years. While I have had ups and downs with my own board, there were many more ups than downs. And I have had the pleasure of associating with many wonderful people on those boards, but nothing is perfect.

There are differences of opinion on this subject, and I admit that I stand with the minority. I can assure you that had most traditional non-profit boards been aware of any of the actions I mentioned in the *Shake It Up, Baby* section before they were executed, they would never have happened. Here is how many non-profit boards handle an innovative idea. First, they form a committee. Then the committee discusses the idea over the course of several meetings. At one of those meetings, they will decide to research other cities to find "best practices". Finally, out of fear of offending the community with a $3.5 million challenge or the Denard CEO by telling him that his position is the main cause of a less-than-stellar campaign, they will kill both ideas.

I firmly believe that when there is no existing barrier to progress, the board or the executive director of a non-profit organization will often create one. With the professionals, fear of moving forward could be caused by the fact that they are so beaten down with rules from government and other funders that they are afraid to be creative. And there are myriad reasons for board members being overly cautious. Their hesitancy could be caused by fear of litigation or fear of making an unpopular decision that could affect their standing in their real jobs. Or they might just plain lack vision. Of course, there's also that human trait of resistance to change that exists in so many. I contend that routinely leaving important decisions totally to a non-profit board is a mistake and a road to mediocrity and chronic status-quo. There needs to be a strong influence by the CEO of the organization.

It is not easy for board members to understand that their job is to partner with the CEO to establish policy, ensure the financial stability of the organization, oversee adherence to applicable laws and ethical standards, make a financial contribution, volunteer to perform a specific task when asked, and advocate for the cause at every practical opportunity. The board has the authority to hire and fire the CEO based on results. If you have hired the right person for the job, get out of the way and let her do it. If you have the wrong person, deal with that.

For-profit boards are usually composed of people who have distinguished themselves in their respective fields. Most meet only once or twice a year. It is common for the CEO to be the board chair. As long as things go well, the board doesn't interfere with the CEO. He is unquestionably in charge. Here is a situation where I encourage the adoption of the for-profit model by non-profit organizations.

There is a wide variety of reasons for people to volunteer to serve on a non-profit board. They might have a passion for the cause or some special ability the organization needs. They might have been asked by a friend or may be desirous of building a resume. They are often people who hold middle-management jobs or lower at their respective places of employment. The majority of the time, there is no one with experience as a CEO.

The agency's CEO and professional staff should be recognized as experts in the work of the organization. The board members are primarily people who give an hour or two a month to the agency and are, for the most part, unaware of the day-to-day issues of the business. They are on the board for a relatively short time and, once gone, they are not accountable for any bad decisions or actions they may have implemented.

# Beware of the Emperor's New Clothes (What We See Isn't Always What It Is)

We live in a data driven time. All of the stakeholders want to "see the data." My mind travels back to my time in manufacturing. If I had a machine that produced 100 widgets an hour, that would be the baseline. Then, if someone showed me a machine that would produce 200 widgets an hour, that would get my attention. The raw materials don't change, and the same operator would be in place. The only variable is the machine. Depending on its cost, I would have to consider buying that machine. Cause and effect have been established.

Foundations and others who hold grant money to give to the most effective programs also want to see the data. Outcome measurements they call them. I support measuring results as best we can. However, in measuring the human condition, we must be careful not to confuse correlation with proven cause and effect.

Let's say a school system is graduating 70% of the students that enter ninth grade in four years. It sets a goal to increase that rate to 85% in five years. The planned solution is to pay teachers on a volunteer basis for two extra hours a day to tutor students who want that service. Foundation X thinks that is a logical approach, and it grants a half-million dollars to implement the program for five years and promises to consider renewal of the grant if the schools reach their goal.

In five years, the graduation rate is still 70%. Obviously, the idea failed. Or did it? Within those five years the following events occurred:

- Cuts in government funding forced the schools to lay off 20% of their teachers. That caused the average class room size to increase from 30 to 37.
- There was a major downsizing by the town's largest employer causing many of the parents to lose their jobs. Many of the high

school age students had to take minimum wage jobs after school to help out, or worse yet, had to drop out of school to become the bread winner. Or maybe the parent's loss of a job just put more stress in the home to the point that the student couldn't concentrate on her studies.

- The budget for law enforcement was reduced. This caused enforcement of domestic violence and deadbeat fathers laws to no longer be high priorities.

Each of these events was a factor that caused some number of students to drop out of school. We don't know what the tipping point was for each of those students, but it is possible that, without the tutoring program, the graduation rate would have dropped to 60% or lower.

The same logic can be applied in reverse to the measurement of programs that appear to be successful. And yet, those with the money stand together and applaud and pour more money into the apparent successes, and they stand together and denounce the apparent failures. All the while they disregard those collateral circumstances that cause the appearance not to be reality.

Non-profit organizations learn what turns funders on and how to present information accordingly. I'm not saying they cheat, but they do learn how to play the game. Those who learn to play the game the best, usually get the money.

# Opinions We Form From a Distance Can Change When We Get Up Close

There are a couple of impressions widely held by those who manage in the for-profit world. I absolutely bought into them during my business career. (1) Non-profit organizations should be managed in the same manner as for-profits. (2) Those who work in the non-profit sector are somehow a little less than those in business or a profession.

Less in what ways? Maybe less ambitious; you might be a little on the lazy side if you are not held to the tough standards of the business and professional sectors. Maybe less tough; they don't have what it takes to handle the pressure of making a profit. Maybe less intelligent; if they were smart, why would they settle for a lower paying job than they could earn in business?

I had an epiphany not too long after my transition. As far as management practices, many should be replicated going from business to charity. But there are many areas in which standard for-profit management actions don't make sense in a non-profit organization and can even be counterproductive.

For openers, there is no demand for profit. Financial stability is still a requirement, but an agency's budget should be set on using its income to provide services within its mission. It's considered smart management to build a rainy day reserve, but if that reserve grows to an amount that is greater than six months of operating expenses, you might want to stop to consider whether you are feeding too much to the reserve and not enough to services.

In businesses that have departments, divisions, or multiple locations, top management can set policies and procedures, and in most cases those are carried out throughout the company. In human services, there might be several agencies in the same community dealing with different aspects of the same problem—homelessness, poverty, addiction, hunger, and the others. We can debate whether that should be the case, but it is what it is. None of them is the boss of any other one.

At United Way, I was often called upon by a board member or donor to tell one of the agencies that we funded what to do. As president of United Way, I had no authority to do that. Actually, any collaboration is strictly voluntary, and each organization has its own board and its own CEO who often protect their turf like a pit bull hanging onto your pants leg. The only hammer is money, and boards are reluctant to cut funding lest that action become a community issue.

Then there's the presence of volunteers. If a human service agency is not using every volunteer it can get its hands on, it is wasting money. An agency should consider finding a volunteer to do mailings, filing, and other such routine duties. There are also a number of higher level jobs that can be handled by volunteers. Depending on the organization and the skill of volunteers who embrace your cause, they might handle bookkeeping, case work that doesn't require a specialized degree, fund raising, and marketing, to mention a few.

Finally, in business you know who your customers and your potential customers are. You know who your suppliers are. And you know the difference between the two. In the non-profit world, your donors and volunteers are both suppliers and customers. You don't need to convince your suppliers to sell to your manufacturing company or your store, but in a non-profit agency, you need to *sell* your potential donors and volunteers on the idea of giving to your organization. That means they are customers in that respect, but they also *supply* the money and volunteer time necessary for you to operate.

When you go to the supermarket, you select and pay for your items and take your groceries home. As a donor to a charity, you pay for the groceries, but someone else takes them to her home. That is a very different dynamic and one that needs to recognized in managing a non-profit organization.

These are huge differences. Every person who agrees to serve on a non-profit board should have an orientation that makes him aware of these differences. Then we could avoid the question so often asked of agency CEO's, "Why don't you run your agency the same way I run my business?" Once that question surfaces, the CEO is forever on the defensive trying to justify her strange methods. Even worse is the scenario where board members think the question but don't ask. Then there can be a continuing suspicion about the quality of the management of the organization without the CEO's awareness.

In reference to the perception of inferiority in the human service world, I wasn't right about that either. The truth is that most of those who choose this direction do it deliberately. They are driven by different motives than the size of their paycheck and their desire to be or to impress a big-shot. After seventeen years, it is my opinion that those employed in both sectors are just about equal in intelligence, drive, and toughness. Just as in the business world, there are highs and lows in each of those qualities, but neither group is noticeably better than the other. They just have different motivations and priorities.

## Volunteers—the Lifeblood the Human Services Industry

Research has proven that, in many agencies, one of the wisest of expenditures is to hire a volunteer-coordinator—someone whose only duty is to recruit, train, supervise, and recognize volunteers. Depending on the size of the agency, this may be a full-time or part-time position. How about a volunteer volunteer-coordinator? That is okay as long as the volunteer is held to the same standards of regular hours and commitment as a paid employee. This work is too often left to whomever on the staff, from the CEO to the receptionist, has time to do it at any given moment. Fact is nobody has time, so it is often done haphazardly. In employing a volunteer coordinator, the agency must maintain the discipline that she is not expected to answer the phone, fill in for the receptionist, file papers, or perform any of the other duties that come up around an office. Once you cross that line, it is a short step until you find that all you have hired is an extra pair of hands, and you are right back where you started in ensuring the proper use of volunteers.

Nothing can turn off a volunteer more than to perceive incompetence on the part of agency to which she has agreed to give her time. What if she has been asked to come to paint a room on a Saturday, only to arrive and discover that no one is there, or no one thought to buy paint? She will probably never be back to your agency and may decide that volunteering, in general, is a waste of her valuable time.

Volunteers need to be treated as the valuable resources they are—not as just a commodity. Give them plenty of pats on the back and occasionally bring in lunch for them. If the agency can afford it, have an annual dinner to celebrate them. If you can't afford it, find a friendly company to sponsor it. Volunteers should receive the same level of respect as your professional colleagues.

## Collaboration—a Vital Component of Human Service Agencies

Fund raising is the top priority of any United Way. However, one of the conditions I had insisted upon when I took the job was that our United Way would not just raise and distribute money. It would become a leader of social change in our community.

Several years before I came to the job, the executive directors of all of the United Way agency members formed a group that met once a month to discuss issues of common interest. They called it the United Way Agency Administrators Council (UWAAC). When I found out about it, I asked if

I could start attending. The agency directors were shocked. Not only had my predecessor never met with them, he was very vocal in his opposition to their existence. My request to join was the beginning of a long and productive partnership with those who actually provided the services with the money United Way raised. Mine was an attitude they had never seen, and most of them were happy about it.

Once a quarter, UWAAC hosted a brown bag lunch to which the directors of all non-profit human service organizations in the county, whether they were affiliated with United Way or not, were invited. I went to my first of those meetings in October 1995. There were six people besides me in attendance. The chairperson of UWAAC was the leader, but there was no agenda. The primary topic discussed was the abolishment of the brown bag event. Since I had been on the job for only two months, I had promised myself that I would just listen. However, given the direction of the discussion, I had to break that promise.

I asked if they would allow me to be responsible for the January, 1996 meeting. That got me a reprieve from the dissolution of the group. I recruited two women, whom I had already observed shared my commitment to lead change, to work with me to plan that meeting. They were Shirley Blaine from Lime-Desmond and Donna Dietrichson. Donna worked at a local financial management company and spent many hours a month in various volunteer roles. She, like Shirley, was not afraid to take me to task when she thought I was off base. She played the role of my conscience to such a degree that I nicknamed her Jiminy Cricket. We added Sandy Marlowe, who had not been at the lunch but was enthralled with the idea, to our planning team. Sandy chaired the First Call for Help board, and she and I had become friends due to her frequent presence in the United Way office building.

One of the problems that I had already noticed in the human services community was that there was a great deal of turf protection. Each agency was so afraid of losing grant money that they often were reluctant to share information and resources with other agencies. Rather than become partners, they became, in effect, adversaries. This approach created a barrier to serving in the best interest of the people in need of their services.

Shirley, Jiminy, Sandy, and I decided to turn the name of the group from the colorless brown bag lunch to the *Dream Team*. We meant for this name to imply that participants would use this forum to dream together as to what could be and then develop action plans to get there. A large assembly room at City Hall was reserved, and we sent out invitations to a four-hour retreat in January. United Way would furnish lunch. Not only the executive directors were invited, but we suggested that they bring key staff personnel and a board member or two. Another of my observations about the non-profit world that I arrived at over the years was, if you feed them, they will come.

To say we were surprised when eighty people from forty-two different agencies showed up is an understatement. We assigned each participant to one of ten tables of eight being careful not to put two representatives of the same agency at the same table. We gave each table a scenario to discuss for an hour. Each topic was designed to produce the outcome of getting participants to know more about agencies other than their own and to create a spark as to how it might be beneficial to work together on some issues. Then, each group was given ten minutes to report out to everyone and five minutes for input from the assembly. Sound familiar? Remember clean-up day at Thursby Plastics? It really worked well. The fences weren't exactly falling like Pompeii in the volcano, but they did appear to be shrinking. More importantly, we had broken the ice on collaboration. That gave us hope for future dialogue among agencies.

The event was successful enough to encourage our intrepid foursome to schedule another session six weeks hence. That one was at the same site for two hours and attracted about sixty people—mostly returnees, but some new blood. Most of the executive directors that had attended the first meeting were there, but many of the staff and board members that had previously accompanied them were not. Here we discussed putting some structure into the informal organization. The desire was to be informal to the point that participation was strictly voluntary, there were no dues, and there was no obligation except that when you attended, you must come with an open mind.

By the end of the meeting, we had created three loose knit components. (1) The *Safety Net* group would focus on those in urgent need—those who were homeless, hungry, jobless, and/or abused. (2) The *Self Sufficiency* component would develop ideas for people whose basic needs were met but who were still largely dependent on the system. (3) The *Community*

*Building* team would find ways for people who had successfully used assistance they had received to give back to the community.

Several tangible and intangible successes came from the Dream Team. The safety net team developed a program called *Wheels-to-Work*. There are many programs throughout the country that allow donors to give used cars that would be sold, usually for scrap, and designate a charity to receive the proceeds. Our program went a step further. It was also based on donated cars, but ones that still had substantial miles left in them.

A corps of volunteers who knew about cars was recruited. Their job was to give a safety inspection to each donated vehicle. If a car was not usable, it was sold for scrap. The proceeds from the sale were used to sustain the program. The usable vehicles were sold to people who needed a car to get either to work or to school. The price was set on what was affordable to the recipient. A local bank stepped up to finance the cars at no interest. As of today, several hundred cars have been and are on the streets, and few have been repossessed. This has clearly been a life-changing program for many of those involved.

The most important initiative that came out of the Dream Team was *Priority One: Put Kids First*. In 1998, we issued a call to all organizations that dealt with young people from birth through high school. In addition to the usual suspects among the human services agencies, representatives of the public and some of the private schools, child care centers and homes, the hospital, law enforcement, the court system, and the welfare department attended.

At the first meeting, there were about seventy-five people around the table. I gave my pitch that the youth population was the community's and the nation's hope for the future. I knew that was not a revelation, especially for the audience to whom I was speaking. But I thought it needed to be said because professionals too often take the routine of their work for granted and forget how essential it is and how vital they are in its execution.

Over time, Priority One created several sub-groups, most of which are still active today. One of those was *Teen Council*. There are three high schools in the county, and this group provided an opportunity for teens to sponsor activities that crossed school lines. Priority One leaders established a small, informal adult advisory team. The advisers let it be known from the beginning that the kids were in charge of developing whatever kinds of activities and programs they wanted.

Of course, as kids, their primary interest was to have fun. In the first year, they sponsored an end-of-school celebration they called the Battle of the Bands. They solicited tapes from bands composed of high school students and invited four of them to perform at the concert. The city park department co-operated in giving them use of a large outdoor amphitheater. The concert was a huge success with over a thousand teens attending. Teen Council took responsibility for security, and there was a minimal amount of trouble.

With that success, Teen Council decided to have a back-to-school concert at the same venue in late August. For this one, the kids used the money they had accumulated from various fund raisers to hire a professional band that had some regional recognition. The winner of the Battle of the Bands opened for them. Again, it was a big success.

The advisers suggested that Teen Council needed to develop a community service arm. The kids soon initiated a teen court with peer judgment and sentencing for first-offense misdemeanors. The court system supported the program and agreed to expunge the records of young people who went through this process, with the provision that the same person could not take advantage of teen court more than once.

Another project Teen Council thoroughly enjoyed was in partnership with Housing Partnerships, Inc. HPI is a local non-profit that buys run-down homes and refurbishes them to sell at affordable prices and low interest to people with moderate incomes. Part of the process is the demolition of the unusable parts of the structure. That could mean walls, windows, kitchen fixtures, flooring, and sometimes even the whole building. What part of HPI's work would a fifteen year old enjoy? Of course, it's the destruction phase. The Housing Partnerships construction director recognized this immediately and established Teen Council members as demolition specialists. They even recruited two volunteers to be foremen. This turned out to be a successful marriage that has worked well for several years.

Teen Council also created a spinoff organization they called VolunTEENS that promotes the availability of all interested teens for various volunteer jobs throughout the community. This has become a popular option for students who have a community service requirement for graduation or for those who have been sentenced to community service for a misdemeanor.

Another component of Priority One, that gave me both pride and frustration, was the *Zero to Eight Council*. I took an inventory in early 2000 and learned that there were eighteen organizations in our county that focused on children somewhere within the ages of 0 to 8. Each dealt with different ages in that spectrum and had different approaches, but I reasoned that there had to be some redundancy; hence, a waste of money and other resources. There had to be room for some collaboration to reduce expenses and increase the capacity and quality of services. Most of the eighteen executive directors agreed that the idea had merit and came to the first meeting.

My frustration came in defining collaboration. The agency leaders thought it meant giving references to other providers and sharing equipment and materials. To me, it meant the merging of agencies. Of course, my interpretation was threatening. Each merger would mean one less director and one less board and some undetermined number of staff reductions.

Some good things came from the group including two mergers that I drove from my position as United Way president. Both suffered through campaigns of letters to the editor published in the newspaper and hate calls to me and others involved. Both the council and I survived, although I pulled out in 2008 feeling that I had given all I had to give. I felt that some of my views had become so controversial that I was more a deterrent than a help to future success.

In 2009, Priority One was dissolved into the Council for Youth Development and lives on with most of the former components and some new ones. It had lasted longer than my seven year theory, but I think the same reasoning applies. Every so often, you have to put on new clothes because your old ones are starting to look shabby.

## The Most Important Issue of Our Time and Why

You may think it presumptuous of me that, of all the work we have to do and problems we have to solve, I would anoint any one item as "*the* most important." Yet after seventy-plus years of observing the world we live in, including the last seventeen dealing with social issues, I am so certain that I am willing to put myself out there. What do you think? Is it the national defense? No—we spend way too much on that already. Is it education? No—that is step two of my issue. Is it climate change? No—although that is high on my list, and if it as serious as some believe, it will trump everything else. Is it homelessness? Hunger? The environment? Unemployment? Equal treatment and acceptance of all people? Terrorism? The growing gap between the haves and have-nots? The growing prison population? Oil? No, no, no, no, no, no, no, no, and no, although every one of those problems requires a huge amount of our attention as soon as possible.

I strongly contend that the number one issue that we need to address with all the vigor and all the resources at our disposal is early child development. On the surface, this seems minor compared to the other possibilities listed. Here is my reasoning. There is indisputable evidence that human brains are 80-90% developed by age three. The necessary wiring is connected in those first three years, and if it doesn't happen by then, the child's potential is greatly reduced. The opportunity is lost; those connections will not happen later in life. By age five, values are formed. Those will be the basis for the child's entire life. It will be determined if he will be honest or devious, industrious or lazy, ethical or deceitful, trusting or defensive, generous or selfish, and all the other characteristics that are relevant to one's makeup. Once the values are ingrained in an individual, it is highly unlikely that she will ever change to any great degree.

To help me to make the case, let me proffer an analogy that goes to back to the beginning of my manufacturing career. At Kane Power Industries, our primary raw materials were large iron castings, which we machined to specifications. They were used as housings for our products. The quality control procedure in 1980 was to machine, let's say, 300 castings in a run. When the run was completed, an inspector, was called in to measure them against specified tolerances and pass judgment as to whether they were acceptable for use. There were three possible results of that inspection. (1) They met specifications and could go to the assembly line. (2) They varied hopelessly from specifications, and they went to the scrap heap. (3) They were close but not quite to specifications. In this instance, they were sentenced to a purgatory we called rework, from which some more machining and labor might save them for use. However, the additional labor cost us any profit that might have been attainable if those castings had been machined correctly in the first place.

In the late seventies and early eighties, American manufacturing began to embrace a quality control technique called *statistical process control*. This procedure called for the machine operator to measure every tenth casting to ensure that it met prescribed tolerances. If the measurement was drifting toward the edge of a given tolerance, he adjusted the machine to bring it back to the middle of the tolerance range. In effect, he measured to predict if he would later produce an unacceptable product. If so, he prevented the making of a reject by adjusting the setup. A little later, we learned that if we went into the foundry of our supplier and imposed some production standards on it, we would prevent the receipt of out-of-tolerance raw castings.

Statistical process control is still used today. It has been enhanced by some other more sophisticated procedures to ensure quality. Together, they lead to earning an ISO certification, which is almost universally demanded of suppliers in the twenty-first century.

So what's the point? In life, our raw materials are infants. The processes to make them a useful product are pre-natal care, parenting, child care, a wholesome and healthy environment, diet, exercise, and various programs that are a positive influence on their development.

Yet, we continue to produce scrap and rework. Children who are raised from birth within the prescribed tolerances usually turn out to be pretty good citizens. They get an education, hold a job, become good parents, and are assets to their community. Those who are raised carelessly are often not ready for kindergarten when the time comes. From there, it's a downward spiral. They aren't equal to the other kids intellectually, socially, and emotionally. Being behind, they become disenchanted with school and often rebel in various ways. This frequently leads to dropping out, unemployment, welfare, trouble with the law, poverty, and on and on. Then they continue the cycle with children of their own.

Are you not yet in agreement with me that this is *the* single most urgent issue of the day? Those children comprise the generation that might solve the other problems I listed. We need to equip today's two-year-olds to be ready to do a better job than we have done. In my opinion, that doesn't set a very high bar. We've worked on these problems for decades with no solutions. We manage the problems as best we can, but we don't solve them. Until we cut off the pipeline of people becoming scrap and rework, we will perpetuate the cycle. The big barrier is that the solution will be horribly expensive. We have to run parallel programs for twenty years while we clear the pipeline of those children we have already mishandled.

We have become a society of short-term thinkers. We are not willing to invest in a product or process that won't pay off for several years. Instead, we put Band-Aids on our existing products, or we make cheap, inferior new products that will break as soon as the warranty expires. That is a practice that leads to mediocrity, which is where we are today.

It is essential that we build a child care system for working parents that is high quality and taught by professionals educated in child care. We also have to make it affordable to all parents. Child care is a common ground where values can be taught.

There are two other traits that are not exactly values. Yet, they are as important as any values we can imagine. Those are intellectual curiosity and hope. We want our children to be insatiable in their thirst for knowledge. And a child without hope is a child lost.

All of these characteristics need to be modeled rather than preached. Many parents don't model any of these traits, because they neither possess nor value them. When that is the case, it has to be done outside the home. Child care is the most likely influence to make a difference. Kindergarten and first grade are too late to be an effective starting point.

We also have to build an enormous parent education network for those parents who are willing to admit that they shouldn't necessarily raise their children as they were raised and are open to learning better methods. By the way, bad parenting crosses all socio-economic lines.

These are not the only actions necessary to turn the ship around, but they will do for a start. I only know that we need to address early child development in a big way, or the products of our education system will continue to deteriorate at an accelerated rate. Proliferation of drop-outs, poverty, crime, and our prison population will continue.

The cost will be in the billions *every* year. Where would the money come from? The only possible answer is tax dollars. You can't pass the hat among individuals and corporations and expect to reap an amount necessary to make a difference. The financing of the solutions has to be mandated. Money could be made available from a major tax increase or from a redeployment of existing dollars. I suggest reducing the bloated defense budget and reallocating the money gleaned from that.

# Please Don't Judge Me to be a Crackpot Just Because of this Next Segment

If you think it's radical to identify child development as our most demanding issue, let me present a crazy idea that will really make your head spin. I will start with the disclaimer that I recognize that what I'm going to propose is so extreme that I will never see it happen, but it should. Discuss among yourselves ideas to see how close we can get to it.

In the early days of America's westward movement, Dad worked the land and Mom stayed home and raised the children. It was decided that when the children reached about the age of six, they would enter a group learning environment called school.

In time, Dad found employment in the city, but Mom was still home, and the school system continued to be sufficient. Then, before we knew it, many Moms were working outside the home. We were introduced to a whole new set of problems that, as a society, we still haven't come close to solving. The need has been exacerbated by the explosion in the number of one-parent households.

Child care became a new industry. Our children up to age nine or ten needed a haven when they were not in school and no parents were home. This industry took a wide variety of forms—grandma, Aunt Minnie, neighbors, child care centers, and homes where the resident has opened a child care business. Some of these facilities were held to various standards, but many were not.

Today there are tens of thousands of people and places that offer one form of child care or another. Some relatives and friends do it for free, but for most venues there is a charge. The cost and quality of these options varies widely, not only from format to format but within a given format.

Some places are safe, but the children are not exposed to developmental activities. I call that a TV, a Pepsi, and a Twinkie. Others are safe and offer age-appropriate activities and nutritional meals. Some are neither safe nor developmental nor healthy. Some facilities are licensed by the state and are held to specified standards. But anyone can open a rogue facility where they are held to no standards.

In most states, you can pay the tuition at your state university for your 19-year-old for less than you can put your 2-year old into full-time day care at a licensed center.

Let me describe what we might do if we could start over with a clean sheet of paper and design a system to accommodate today's lifestyle. As you read it, it will become obvious that this is about as pie-in-the-sky as one can get, but please dream along with me for a minute.

- Offer public school, ***on an optional basis***, beginning at age six-months. Of course, the first few years would be the equivalent of child care.
- Today's mandatory rule of entering kindergarten at five would still be in place, but before that, parents would have a choice. Families in need of child care could exercise the in-school option and be certain that their children were receiving safe, clean, developmental care with nutritional meals.
- The care givers would be educated in their profession so that the care would be reasonably consistent. Employment would require at least a two-year degree in child care or teaching.
- Generate funds by charging those who can afford it for the pre-kindergarten years. Use a sliding scale ranging from free to the very low income people to full cost for those who have incomes over a certain amount.
- Offer discounts for multiple children from the same family.

You say, "Gee, Joe, this makes so much sense, why don't we just do it?" Since the rules on teacher to child ratio are more stringent for younger children, the cost of public education would skyrocket. Also, we would need an investment to expand our facilities to accommodate the increased number of children in the schools. This "crazy" idea would cost billions more annually than my first alternative.

Please let me know the name of any politician who wants to present this idea to Congress. I promise this chapter will be the first, last, and only political statement you will read in this book. But I must say that implementation of this idea would be the ultimate **Machete Moment.**

# What Have I Done about It?

In 2000, as part of Priority One, I launched an effort I called *100 Meetings in 100 Days.* The subject of the meetings was child and youth development. I visited the editor of the local newspaper to enlist his help in getting the word out about the program. From February first through early May, I committed to going to any group that would let me in. It could be any time and at any venue. There, I would lead a discussion on whatever facet of the topic the assembly wanted to discuss. The editor told me that I was out of my mind to make such a commitment and, at my age, I wouldn't hold up. I told the editor just to publicize the offer, and I would take care of the rest, including my own well-being.

The theme of the program was, *Make Sierra County the best place in America to raise a kid or to be a kid.* The format was that I would make a presentation that would fit the time the host allotted. As it played out, my time parameters were anywhere from fifteen minutes to an hour. Thirty-minutes was the most common timeframe. I took a flip chart that had been marked off in sections. Across the top were the age groups: infants, toddlers, pre-school, and elementary, middle, and high school. Down the side were parenting, child care, school, peers, religion, and programs—the major influences in a young person's development. After sizing up the audience, I made a presentation I thought would be tailored to that crowd. I usually took about one-third of the allotted time, not exceeding fifteen minutes, for the presentation. I then asked the participants to take the lead in whatever part of the chart in which they were most interested. I recorded every comment and question in the appropriate block(s) on the chart.

The response was extremely encouraging. All of the service clubs called. I figured they were always looking for speakers to fill their programs and would take anyone available. But I learned that many of their members, especially those who were parents, were truly interested in the subject. I visited about every type of organization you might imagine—PTA's, school staffs, high school and college classes, work places, departments of local government, community betterment groups, Sunday School classes, and human service organizations.

One of my favorite stories came from a call I received from what sounded like an elderly woman. She wanted me to speak at her KKK meeting. I didn't think the only KKK I knew about would be interested in my views on child development, but I had said "any group", so I stayed on the phone. We agreed on a date, and the meeting would be at 7:30 PM. It gets dark about six o'clock that time of year in Indiana. She told me that the house where the meeting would be held was out in the country and would be hard for me to find. She suggested that we meet at the Marathon station at the intersection of two rural highways. Then, I could follow her to the site. This was getting scarier by the minute, but I agreed to meet her.

We met as planned, and I followed her from the station for about a mile when she turned onto a gravel path. After about two miles on the gravel, she stopped in front of an ordinary looking home. I was looking for an escape route, just in case my worst fears were realized. I was encouraged when I didn't see any burning crosses. Upon entering the home, I found ten women, none of whom were south of sixty-five years old, and none of whom were wearing sheets over their heads. I was relieved to hear them explain that KKK stood for Kitchens-Kindness-Karing. When the group had formed thirty years ago, they thought KKK would be catchy. I believe these women were so innocent that they knew no of other use of their acronym. The club's primary purpose was to meet once a month and organize projects to help the church and the school and to exchange recipes. As it turned out, we met for over an hour, and it was one of the most productive meetings of the series. It's amazing how one's imagination can run wild upon hearing a certain term.

Priority One installed a large bulletin board type scoreboard in the common area of a downtown mall. By large, I mean huge. This thing was every bit of 12 feet high by 16 feet wide. It was laid out in the same format as the flip-chart pages on which I took the notes. Every few days, I posted the comments from recent meetings on the board. I condensed ones that were similar, and as a given comment or question became more frequent or was said more passionately, I increased the size of the font and then went to colors. A big font in red was meant to get the ultimate attention.

I was pleased to see and hear of many people actually stopping to study the board.

At the end of the hundred days, I invited the community to a wrap-up meeting in the public gathering area of the downtown mall. About 200 people attended and took part in condensing the ideas to develop an action plan. We came up with sixteen action items and appointed a volunteer champion for each. A three-month long **MACHETE MOMENT.**

One action that genuinely resonated with me and many others was the result of a question asked by a factory worker at one of the PTA presentations. He asked, "How can we deal with the conflict between the two most important jobs a person holds in life—the one we get paid for and being a parent?"

He was uncommonly perceptive in his basis for the question. With many employers, there was no forgiveness for missing an hour or a day of work to tend to parental duties. I championed that one myself, and I actually believe we moved the needle. I conducted several one-on-one and group meetings with local CEO's and HR directors to make my case. The combination of my contacts in the manufacturing fraternity and my acceptance as a leader of social change made business leaders inclined to take my call. Whether it was a result of Priority One's efforts or just a change in what is acceptable in society, I will never know. I do know that policies in many workplaces, at least in Sierra County, have become more lenient for those with parenting duties that occasionally conflict with their work.

Several of the action items dealt with expanding awareness of available assistance. The roots of the 0 to 8 group came from here. A junior mentoring program took legs and is still functioning. There is nothing a fourth-grader treasures nothing more than having a high school student pay attention to her.

The most disappointing results came from ideas related to parent training. Priority One called three different well publicized meetings at times and locations convenient to most. A total of eight parents turned out, and they were all people that, judging from their questions and comments, were already good parents looking for ideas to become even better. The lousy parents didn't show up, either because they didn't know they were lousy parents or because they just didn't give a damn. It's not difficult to point to hundreds of parents in our own community who sit in front of the television six hours every night in their dirty houses with a beer in one hand and a cigarette in the other. An example of this ilk was a man who attended one of my presentations at a small machine shop. After listening to my pitch, he told me, "The only time my Dad paid attention to me was to beat me. No one helped me with my homework. I dropped out of school in the eighth grade, and I turned out okay." Yeah, okay!

There were a few of the action items that I could have predicted would fizzle. See teen night club. I have never seen that concept work for more than a few months. The leaders graduate without creating a line of succession. The kids are fickle and become disinterested in doing the same thing for long. If it's a place the parents approve of, there is no point in going because there is no rebellion in that, and if parents don't approve, it is off limits.

The Hundred/Hundred meetings were the most dramatic example of my efforts to lead the community in pushing early child development to the forefront of our social issues. I continued to chair the Priority One group and to advocate for better education of child care providers, higher standards in the child care industry, and making more money available for child care assistance for those who can't afford to pay full price. My advocacy became so persistent that I swear that people were ducking into doorways when they saw me coming down the street.

While I am frustrated that more people didn't fall in line on this issue, I do see our county being ahead of the curve. Our local education coalition, a powerful group made up of educators and community shakers and movers, changed its target population to start at birth rather than Kindergarten. The public school system is now pushing an agenda that makes attention to pre-school children a priority. A new agency was formed to train employees of child care centers and those who offer home care. That agency also develops and enforces local standards for the child care industry. The leaders of every one of those initiatives credit Priority One as the primary early influence in their thinking and as an active partner in getting their particular program off the ground.

# The Seven Year Itch Strikes Again

By 2002, I had been at United Way for seven years. Was it time for a change? I thought so, but this time I got the opportunity to reinvent myself within the same job. For several years, the merger of Munsey Industries with Ugarte Manufacturing in Minnesota had been evolving. Most of Munsey's executives and other top talent had been moved from Vienna to the Ugarte headquarters in St. Paul. The building that once housed several hundred office employees at Munsey corporate headquarters had become a mere shadow of its former self. The lab building across the street was already closed.

In one of the first meetings of human service organizations I attended in 1995, I heard of the desire to have a single place where many human service agencies could be located. This concept made perfect sense. Poor people who needed services tended not to have reliable transportation. More often than not, if they needed one service, they needed multiple ones. We thought it would be ideal if they could go to a single site and have many of their needs tended to in one visit. Plus the co-location concept could facilitate collaboration among the case managers of the tenant agencies.

In 1999, I went to George McPherson, who had been CEO of Munsey Industries and now was COO of the Munsey-Ugarte. I observed that Munsey would have vacated their office building soon and that George would have a white elephant on his hands. He would have two obvious options, both costly. Munsey could either maintain the vacant buildings, or tear them down, and clean up the site. I offered him a third alternative by asking him to consider donating the entire property to United Way to be used as a co-location of human service organizations. George seemed to agree that it was a good idea and promised to get back to me if the time were ever right. For two years, Munsey continued to use a small part of the building, but they were down to about thirty employees at that location. This was another potential move I neglected to run by the board members during its early stages for fear they would throw it into their machinery and kill it.

Meanwhile, George had left the company as the promise for him to be promoted to CEO within a year had not materialized. On his way out, he had apparently remembered my request because, in the spring of 2001,

I got a call from Bob Raven of Munsey. Bob had been given the thankless task of wrapping up Vienna operations for Munsey-Ugarte. He told me to have a business plan for the non-profit use of the property on his desk in sixty days, or he would bring in the wrecking ball. That made twice in my career I had been threatened with a wrecking ball. I submitted the plan in fifty-nine days, and a month later Munsey-Ugarte signed the building over to United Way. A **MACHETE MOMENT.**

The property was six acres with a city street running through the middle. There were three buildings. The main office building on the south side of the street was on two levels plus a basement and contained a total of about 140,000 square feet. On the north side of the street, there was a parking lot of about two acres. The old lab building of 11,000 square feet sat at the rear of the parking lot. And there was an old firehouse (circa 1920) on a corner directly across from the main building. A park-like area of a little less than two acres rounded out the property on the northwest corner. United Way eventually used it as a venue for campaign kickoffs and celebrations in good weather, but that happened only once or twice a year.

My task was to figure out a way to attract non-profit tenants from which we could collect enough rent revenue to enable the property to break even. United Way had some advantages in not having stockholders who demand a profit and in having no mortgage. That allowed us to offer rent that was considerably lower than market price. Agencies were located throughout the city and county. Often, they were in buildings that were in a state of disrepair and in undesirable locations because that was all they could afford. It was common for their quarters to be cramped with too many employees and volunteers for the space.

I started with the large agencies—those that had the potential to become "anchor stores." I asked them to gather information related to their total cost of occupancy—rent, utilities, indoor and outdoor maintenance, trash hauling, phones, and snow removal. The next question was, "What if you could move to a co-location of many agencies in space much more attractive than you have now at no more than your current total cost?" While most were skeptical, when pushed, the vast majority agreed that would be a great opportunity.

I stressed upon them not to enter into any new lease agreements without checking with me. The big breakthrough was with the executive director of the Agency on Aging, which employed about fifty people. She said that she would move as soon as the space could be ready. As a result of that early commitment, I saw to it that her agency got 15,000 ground floor square feet in the front with windows on two sides. She was quickly followed by the executive director of the county welfare office who got the same deal with 20,000 square feet on the second floor.

The welfare department is part of state government. As such, they were willing and able to pay a higher per-square-foot price than other non-profit organizations. (That fact is surely indicative of waste in government spending, but I wasn't going to stir up dust at that point.) They had already been paying a fairly high price at their old site, so to charge what they had been paying allowed me to keep my promise to the others. The welfare department provided a de facto subsidy for the other agencies. Soon, we got commitments from the local domestic violence agency to move their administrative offices out of their shelter and into our main building.

The board and I spent considerable time in one of our monthly meetings trying to come up with just the right name for our new facility. Several ideas surfaced including the Community Services Building. I insisted that if United Way was going to do the work of pulling this concept together and maintaining the property, United Way was sure as hell be part of the brand. In a short time, a large family counseling agency and other smaller agencies committed, and the United Way Center was going to become a reality.

Of the 140,000 square feet in the main building, we were looking to rent only about 80,000 of it. There was a basement not ready for offices, a shipping dock area, an unfinished warehouse section, corridors, stairwells, and rest rooms. And I wanted to build several conference rooms to allow community meetings and board meetings of our tenant agencies. My vision was to have this complex become *the* primary location for gatherings geared to the good of the community. That vision has been fulfilled.

There is a second-hand non-profit store in town, Good Stuff Cheap (referred to by the locals a GSC). Anyone can shop there for clothing, furniture, and household goods—similar to Goodwill. It was located in about 4000 square feet of cramped space near the downtown. It was on a busy street and had a narrow driveway, which made it dangerous for donors and shoppers to get in and out. The store had had to move three times in the past five years because they either their lease had expired, or the space had become totally inadequate.

I stopped there one day early in the process before the Munsey offer was widely known in the community, and asked the director, Jane Boswell, to take a ride with me. She was about 65 years old and had been with the agency since its inception in 1973. This store was her life. I took her to what had been the lab building on the new site. This was a simple block building of 11,000 square feet all on street level with two overhead doors that could be used for dropping off clothing and furniture donations. It sat on the back of the parking lot about a hundred yards from the main building. I told her that this was her new home. She asked what I meant. I explained that this could be the new home of Good Stuff Cheap and that she would never again have to worry about overcrowded space or the safety of people getting in and out. She hugged me and started sobbing. She said that this was the answer to her lifelong dream.

In a few days, after she got over her shock, Jane and I started discussing the potential benefits and making plans for the move and the use of the building. Jane, who had been in poor health for some time, oversaw the move. And then in a few months, her dream fulfilled, she retired.

When Jane announced her impending retirement, I went to the GSC board chair and recommended my old friend and colleague, Bill Muldoon, for the job of executive director. I knew that he had found another job after leaving Thursby, but he was quite unhappy in it. Despite the fact that the GSC job paid much less than his old job at Thursby, the chance to use his management and organizational skills in an entirely new industry intrigued him. He accepted the position and stayed for five years before moving on to a teaching gig at the local college. During Bill's administration, GSC went on to become one of the strongest non-profit agencies in the community. It more than tripled the annual donation/sales activity and added a job training program for rehabilitating felons and others who were previously judged to be unemployable.

Clients of agencies who come to the main building for services often take the opportunity to cross the street to pick up items they need. United Way has established a need-based voucher system for which a person can qualify, depending on her income, to shop at GSC at prices anywhere from zero to half of list price. A person living below poverty level is given a large garbage bag once a quarter. Everything she can stuff into it is free. Transients can have a bag one time. The marriage of this agency to the co-location site was an absolute home run.

# A New and Unusual Challenge—Disaster Recovery

It was 2008. United Way had just completed its first three-and-a-half-million dollar campaign. Everything was rosy, except I felt restless. It had been six years since United Way had acquired the buildings. I needed a new dragon to slay, but I had no new ideas. Continuing normal growth and routine success were not what I was here for. I was faced with chasing mice.

In June, what did we get? We got eleven inches of rain in five hours in the counties upstream from us. With it, came what is known as a hundred-year flood. Floods are labeled according to their predictable frequency. I'm not sure the weather people ever decided whether this was a hundred or a five-hundred year event. All I know is that there was water where water had never been before in my lifetime or in the memory of any of my fellow citizens. Witnesses who were sitting on their porches during the rain described the oncoming water as looking like a small tsunami.

Hundreds of homes were flooded, many beyond repair. Patients were airlifted from our hospital to hospitals in surrounding counties. Schools and businesses were buried in water on their lower levels. Red Cross set up emergency shelters anywhere they could find a dry building.

Obviously, this is not something I had hoped for, but since it happened, I jumped into the fray. As suddenly as the water rose, I had a purpose again. The flood was on a Saturday, and transportation throughout the county was virtually shut down. Several islands had been formed, each cut off from the others. By Sunday noon, the waters were subsiding, and one-by-one the police were opening roads.

As might be expected, actions were disjointed and intense. Everyone wanted to help, but there was no organization to the effort. Some residents just went into neighborhoods and started cleaning up. The city safety director set up an ad hoc committee of community leaders and representatives of several human service organizations. A group of six pastors organized an open meeting to start to plan actions for cleanup.

Kate and I had been marooned in town and ended up sleeping in my office. We had been at a downtown restaurant and, disregarding the flash flood warnings as we are wont to do, had decided to have one for the road. After trying several exits from town, we went to the United Way Center which was six blocks from where we had eaten. In the morning, I took Kate home and returned to the building to do whatever I could to help. I thought that our building would be a logical haven for folks who didn't know where to go.

I was correct, and when I arrived Maggie Hunt was already there. I had recently appointed Maggie to the position of executive director of the Volunteer Action Center (VAC), a division of our United Way. VAC's mission is to recruit and connect residents who want to volunteer with agencies that need help. I didn't know Maggie very well, but that was to change quickly in the crisis. By noon, we had been joined by about two-dozen people who were a mixture of displaced residents and volunteers.

Within minutes on the morning after the flood, Maggie and I decided that the United Way Center lobby was going to be the focal point for volunteers. Of course, we had no authority to make that decision. We just did it, and it stuck. I underestimated the magnitude of the job ahead and went out to buy a cell phone, which was to be dedicated to calls about the flood cleanup and recovery. By Tuesday, there had been six phone lines installed in the lobby, and the cell phone was a thing of the past. The number of calls on both sides of the volunteer/victim equation was overwhelming, and the lobby was packed with victims and people either already involved or wanting to be involved in the cleanup.

Maggie was terrific. She invented a system on the fly to handle volunteers efficiently. One of her first actions was to recruit the first six women who appeared to have any interpersonal skills to work the lobby. She sat them at a table to register people, and on Tuesday she gave each of them one of the new phones. I don't know what these women had in mind when they volunteered, but many of them worked more than one day a week for several months. Maggie recruited more volunteers to handle the phones. We wanted all of them to be answered from 8 to 5.

She assigned me the job of ice man. Each morning by seven o'clock,

I was to bring four twenty-pound bags of ice to the building, empty yesterday's melted ice from the coolers, and stock them with fresh drinks and ice for volunteers to enjoy during their work day. For this, I became known as Iceman throughout the recovery. Some volunteers didn't know me by any other name.

By Monday, the word was out nationwide, and the response was unbelievable. Groups began to arrive, not only from Indiana and contiguous states, but from as far away as Utah and Connecticut. FEMA, which had taken such a bad rap for its performance after Katrina, was on hand early and did a great job for us. I think that was after they had rid themselves of George W.'s buddy, whose credentials were that he had run horse shows.

From Sierra County's perspective, we had no complaints about FEMA. Others on the scene early were volunteers from the Billy Graham Foundation, Samaritan's Purse, INVOAD (the Indiana arm of a nation faith-based disaster organization), and many more. Most were from faith-based organizations, but there were also groups from colleges, service clubs, and just plain people who organized themselves to go help where it was needed. Many families took on the project as a family event. One family even made it a reunion with segments of the family coming from St. Louis, Pittsburgh, and rural Kentucky as well as Vienna. It was thrilling to see how many people were selfless enough to come to our town and help when we, absolute strangers to them, needed it.

There are three distinct steps in dealing with a disaster. Within a given community, there is an overlapping of steps, but there is a clear difference. The first response is to ensure that everyone is safe. In our case, that component was led by the Red Cross, which performs that role in most disasters everywhere. This work is usually pretty short-term.

First response is closely followed by cleanup, the first part of which is muckin' and guttin'. I must admit this was a new term to me. It pertains to cleaning up the mud in the house and carrying all of the ruined items, including the walls, to the street to be thrown away.

Everything porous that got wet has to be thrown away. Even if you dry it, mold will form, and that will create a health problem, not only to the residents of the house affected, but in the neighborhood. That means that not only the furniture and carpets have to go, the wallboard has to be stripped, and in some instances the framing must be torn down.

The pastors group held another meeting on Monday. By this time, there was more awareness of their existence, and the room was full of victims, volunteers, media, and other interested parties. I went early and asked if I could join their leadership team, which they had already dubbed the "steering committee." They seemed happy to get me. Talk about a fish out of water! There I was with six preachers, and I with absolutely no religious convictions.

They gave me one humbling surprise. I had been president of United Way in their community for thirteen years. There was something about United Way and me in the newspaper at least once a month. People I don't even know speak to me wherever I go. And yet, not one of the pastors had ever heard of me. I concluded that those in their profession are so involved with and dedicated to their own congregations and causes that they don't have time to look beyond those into the community. I think that is neither a good thing nor a bad thing. It's just the way it is—at least in Sierra County, Indiana.

Within ten days, it was apparent that a single leader of the flood cleanup and subsequent recovery was needed and that none of the preachers wanted the job. In addition, none of them was connected enough to the necessary resources to do it effectively. I had both qualifications plus a great amount of experience with crisis management from my earlier life. I volunteered to be the director of the flood recovery, and they quickly accepted the offer.

My own board was less than thrilled when I told them of the new role I had taken on without asking them. "Who's going to manage United Way?" "I am." "Won't some of the work be neglected?" "No!"

I continue to be insulted when people who don't know what they are talking about underestimate me. It's not as if I have a long string of failures for them to point at. By now, you have probably figured out that of my many shortcomings, lack of ego and self-esteem are not on the list. That's another reality that I don't consider good or bad. Sometimes people are turned off by it, but then I am often turned off by timidity and lack of action. It takes all kinds to make up a society.

A week into the cleanup, we identified eight major geographical sections of the county that were hit hard and several other areas with lesser damage. We assigned volunteers to teams that would be sent to a specific home or block of homes. That assignment would be that team's project until it was either completed or the volunteers' time to stay had expired. Two of the areas were large mobile home parks.

I soon learned of a few problems, which Maggie took care of at once. In response to some reports of looting, Maggie devised a wristband system to identify authorized volunteers who had registered at United Way Center. The local police were tuned in to the system and found it quite helpful.

Maggie's gang and I needed to have some fun to keep our sanity and senses of humor through this mess. We decided that a good diversion would be to create some ironic groupings among the volunteers. Maggie sent a group of Amish folks from northern Indiana out to work with a group from a synagogue in Louisville. A busload of students from the University of North Carolina partnered with a senior citizens group from Michigan to clean up one of the mobile home parks. The Carolina kids came back three weeks later, and this time Maggie sent them out with another busload from the University of Louisville. They got along just fine as long as they didn't debate who had the better basketball team. I think her best match might have been a Southern Baptist Church from Hazard, Kentucky, with an Italian-American social club from Chicago.

But you know what came from our little sociological experiment? Nothing! There was not one negative incident. We would have heard if there had been because there were several supervisors in each of the affected areas. The supervisors were there to ensure safety, to make certain the necessary tools were available, and to direct work and answer questions.

Not only were there no serious conflicts, there were many reports of volunteers exchanging email addresses and phone numbers with their work mates. I have often wondered if any of those relationships continued in the months and years since the flood.

In that first week or so, there seemed to be one meeting or another every hour or two. Each had several common participants, and each dealt with a different segment of our population. None of us had ever done this before, and we all wanted to do everything we could to fix the problem as quickly as possible. The city safety director hosted a meeting City Hall every morning at 8 o'clock. Soon, the preachers and I were functioning as the steering committee of what we had named the Sierra County Long-Term Flood Recovery Team.

In talking with some of the flood experts who visited us in the beginning, we learned that there is a predictable chronology of emotions, attitudes, and events in a disaster. Immediately, people are in shock. The victims want to save their families, their property, and their belongings. The non-victims want to help. The problem is omnipresent—visible in any direction one might drive. Then in four to six weeks, the visibility wanes. There is no more mud in the streets, and the trash at the curbs has been hauled away. Conversation among those who were not directly affected diminishes. It is replaced by talk about their jobs, kids, teams, etc. Those people don't have the ravaged neighborhoods in their paths as they travel to work, school, or the mall. The influx of first responder organizations has moved on to the next disaster.

This is the moment at which local leadership must take hold. Several actions took place in those first few weeks that put our community in a position to fly on its own.

- The pastors on the steering committee gave us access to a large volunteer population through their churches. They encouraged volunteering at all of their services. This kept the volunteer pipeline flowing longer than it might have.

- The management of the hospital, even though it was shut down, decided to keep everyone on the payroll at full salary for the duration of the recovery. This turned out to be a really big deal. There were 1500 employees, of which only a relatively small percentage could work on the hospital's cleanup and recovery. With no patients, this meant the hospital could make a thousand people available to work on various aspects of the cleanup and recovery throughout the community.

- Lilly Endowment, the philanthropic arm of Eli Lilly Corporation, which is headquartered in Indianapolis, granted $45 million to be used for recovery related to all Indiana disasters in 2008. This grant would be administered by the Indiana Association of United Ways (IAUW). $10 million would go to Red Cross with the remainder to be distributed by IAUW. In addition to the flood in our county, many counties in the state shared the same experience. Plus, there had been an earlier less devastating flood in the northern part of the state and a couple of tornadoes.

Maggie commented that nurses from the hospital were their patients' case managers and, with minimum training, could become case managers to flood victims. This brilliant observation allowed access to a cadre of smart people with experience in managing the crises of individuals. The hospital assigned twelve nurses to work full time as flood recovery case managers at United Way Center.

When the committee at IAUW reviewed the needs across the state, we were granted $1.7 million to fund recovery for individual home-owners and small businesses, and the hospital received another $6 million.

# Success through People—Many Professionals and Many Many Volunteers

In the first month, the focus was entirely on cleanup. The recovery team had not yet developed a strategy for the long-term recovery. We had to use our resources to put first things first, and that meant getting well into the cleanup before we dealt with the long-term. We informed the community of our priority and that we would get to the recovery as soon as it was practical to do so. However, that delay allowed rumors to become rampant as to what would happen beyond cleanup. The daily meetings at City Hall continued for the first two weeks, but they too were about cleanup. A couple colleagues and I represented United Way and the Long-Term Recovery Team at those meetings. Those two entities had become synonymous in people's minds. The usual cast of city and county officials was present at the meetings along with FEMA and the other helping organizations as long as they were in town. Of course, the predictable number of local politicians, congressmen, and legislators dropped by to pledge their support. One congressman even cried when he spoke of seeing the devastation in the neighborhood in which he had grown up. I will never believe those weren't crocodile tears, but I admit to being cynical when it comes to politicians.

While the morning meetings had been invaluable in the first ten days, attendance began to decline as assignments were completed, and within another week, that meeting ceased to exist. That was not bad thing because we had reached the point of too many meetings, often producing conflicting information. It was around the Fourth of July that the recovery segment began to take shape.

We identified three major components as essential to the recovery—volunteer coordination, case management, and construction. I recruited a manager for each component who would join me on the management committee of the Long-Term Flood Recovery Team. The volunteer manager was easy. Maggie had entrenched herself in that job from day one.

Within a day after the nurses had reported for duty, Sherry Bannister, who was the daytime charge nurse on the fourth floor of the hospital, distinguished herself as the leader of her peers. During the training session to transition their skills to flood-specific problems, she was the first to understand. In fact, within an hour, she had transformed herself from trainee to trainer. Sherry accepted my invitation to be the Case Management Manager.

I had to look outside for the Construction Manager. It was time to reach back twenty years. I knew that Jack McCloud had parted ways with Lund Construction. Jack was a good-old- boy who was always quick with a smile and a joke. I think our attraction to each other was that we were both wise-asses who disdained authority figures that were too full of themselves. In the ensuing twenty years, I had run into Jack about a dozen times in grocery stores and bars. On those occasions, we always shared a laugh and then went our own ways until we met again. But recently, I always had sensed that Jack was covering up some depression with a faux happy-go-lucky attitude. I suspected that the cause was that he didn't have a regular job.

In my most recent contact with Jack, about a year earlier, I learned that he was no longer with Lund and was doing occasional jobs he could pick up on his own. I called him to come in for a talk. Meanwhile, Maggie told me that she had met Jack when he came in to volunteer for flood work. She, being unaware of his experience and skills, had assigned him to a muckin' and guttin' crew, and he had readily accepted that work. When he visited me, Jack jumped at the chance to have full-time work for an estimated two years as the working manager of the recovery construction team. He would recruit his own crew and be paid 32 bucks an hour. His crew would receive $20 to $28 depending on their skills.

It was now late July, six weeks after the event. The muckin' and guttin' work was winding down. I had my management team and knew how much money we had to work with. We were ready to fly. I asked the media to publicize a community meeting that would be held on August first in the high school auditorium. The newspapers and radio stations responded enthusiastically with banner headlines and lead stories in every newscast. If I were reading this as one who had not been involved, I would think that seven weeks between the flood and the big informational meeting regarding recovery was an unreasonably long time. Believe me. It could not have been done any faster. We were not ready for long-term recovery until all the first response work was completed and we were well along in the cleanup.

By then, the three recovery components had their members identified so that they could hit the ground running as soon as the community meeting was behind us. I had begun to have regular meetings of the management team (the three function managers and I) on Mondays and Thursday at 8 AM. These were essential early on because the three functions shared the same cases from different perspectives.

It can be argued that the use of tee shirts in America has become overdone. It seems that every time you go for a walk, it's for a cause, and you get a tee shirt. On the other hand, it gives us a chance to tell the world what team we root for, what charities we give to, or that we are proud grandmas.

I thought this was a time when tee shirts would serve a real purpose. I designed a shirt that you couldn't miss. It was bright red with large white letters, Sierra County Long-Term Flood Recovery Team. Two days before the meeting, I coaxed a local sporting goods store to print a hundred of them on short notice and have them to me before the three o'clock meeting. At 2:45 the shirts were delivered outside the auditorium.

All of those who were to be on stage were assembled in a classroom which we used as the school's version of a green room. There was the entire Flood Recovery Team, which now numbered twelve with some additions I had recruited so that I would not be so overwhelmed by the religious contingent. Also, there were the management team, two FEMA reps, a Small Business Administration spokesperson, a congressional aide, and a governor's representative.

We gave everyone except the politicians a shirt and told them that they had to wear it in order to be on stage. The men who had worn dress shirts and ties could wear it over their shirts. The priest on the steering committee wore his over his collar. Women who had dressed up for the event could cover their fancy clothes with their shirts, but we were all going to wear them. The impression I was bent on making was to ensure the community that there was an organized effort to help them out of the mess. The words *long-term* and *team* were deliberately chosen. Long-term said we were on the job until it was done, and team implied that this was not just a committee, which can be perceived as a small group that accomplishes little and disbands prematurely.

Twenty chairs were lined up across the stage. The crowd numbered about seven-hundred. There was a large contingent of flood victims. Our ushers directed them to sit together in one section. The rest of the audience was made up of government officials, media, and just plain citizens, most of whom were volunteering in some way. The case managers, in their red shirts, sat as a group in the front row. This was a moment everyone had been waiting for.

The team and I all walked onto the stage together and stood for a moment. The politicians obeyed my instruction to take the last two seats away from the podium. The audience reaction was something none of us had anticipated. There was a prolonged silence, I think while they read the shirts, followed by loud applause. It was if they had seen the first reason to think there might be an end to their nightmare. I wasn't alone in not being unable to choke back tears.

Then, the others all took their seats while I opened the meeting. As my opening address, I shared the following information, plans, and promises:

- While I hoped that this would be the meeting to end all meetings, I was sure that it would not be.
- The people in the red shirts would not rest until the recovery job was done.
- The structure and purpose of the steering committee and the management team.
- The function of the case managers whom I asked to stand. The case managers would be seated at a long table in the lobby and were

prepared to serve victims after the meeting. For those who already had a case file open, the case manager would update the file and answer questions. For those who were seeing a case manager for the first time, a file would be opened. For both existing and new clients, appointments could be made for an in-depth conversation either in the case management office or at the flood site.

- None of the team would leave the auditorium until every one of the victims' questions had been answered to the best of our ability. In some cases, the answer would be, "We don't know, but we will find out and get back to you." In those instances, we took names and contact information.
- The media had volunteered to publish daily updates, and there would be a weekly meeting at the Disciples of Christ Church as long as those meetings remained meaningful.

We set a minimal number of ground rules for the meeting. Everyone on stage would remain after the meeting to answer questions that were specific to a single property. I asked those with questions that were unique to their situation to use that forum so that they would not tie up everyone's time for issues that were not of concern to multiple people in the audience. In the same vein, I reserved the right to cut off anyone who was monopolizing the time. I deliberately did not outlaw anger, although we were prepared to deal with anyone who got out of hand. This turned out to be a good decision because a significant number of victims were angry, and many didn't know for sure at whom, so they took it out on whoever was available.

I then introduced the members of the Long-Term Recovery Team, the experts from afar, and the politicians. It was time to turn the podium over to one of the FEMA reps. She presented valuable information about what victims could expect from FEMA and how they could access FEMA's help. She pointed to our case management operation as the place to go when they had questions. The Small Business Administration representative explained, in detail, how to obtain an SBA loan. She also clarified that the word "business" in their name was not meant to imply that individuals were not eligible. And a representative of Indiana government told of some assistance available through the state.

The rules for accessing FEMA and SBA were clearly defined. Flood victims were required to apply for a FEMA grant and an SBA loan. Whatever money they received from those sources had to be used for their personal flood recovery. Then they could come to the Long Term Recovery Team, and a case manager would review their situation with a bias toward covering the remaining cost to make them whole. We gave the case managers considerable autonomy in those decisions, but some situations were so gray that they had to come before the management team.

That was enough speaking. We were there to listen to the victims' questions and needs. So we opened the gates, and the questions rolled in. Most of the comments and questions were pretty civil. However, there was some rage over what had or, more often, had not been done to date. Some of the anger was well directed about mistakes or omissions that had occurred. As we had agreed before the meeting, the team did not make excuses. We simply apologized and promised to correct any mistakes as soon as possible. Of course, in a situation as intense as the flood recovery, mistakes and omissions are bound to happen, but when they happen in your case, understanding is not easy to come by.

All victims were encouraged to stay to talk with any member of the recovery team. If the person they were talking with could not help, they would be taken to someone who had the knowledge and authority to give the necessary assistance. Most of the victims appreciated the time and interest we were taking. Of course, there are some people you just can't please. Even with the crankiest of clients, the team members did the best they could to be patient and serve them.

Maggie's original volunteer management group transitioned from coordinating volunteers for cleanup to assigning jobs for recovery. Three of the women assisting her with volunteers were working so many hours that the management team felt it was only right to put them on the payroll. We settled on a stipend of $10 an hour for any member of the volunteer team who regularly worked over 10 hours in a week. Most of the others were working either one 8-hour day or two 4-hour days, and none of them thought that policy was unfair. They all said that they intended this as a volunteer activity and didn't expect to be paid. On the other hand, the three who were working 30 to 40 hours a week really appreciated the gesture. One of them became a permanent employee of the Volunteer Action Center and is still there today.

Sherry had a full complement of case managers, twenty-seven in all. The twelve from the hospital were all outstanding. We had predicted that, based on the nurses' case management experience working with patients, and we were not disappointed. The other seventeen were of mixed quality, ranging from excellent to incompetent. About a half-dozen saw their role as telling flood victims how to straighten out their lives, rather than focusing on listening to their clients' needs and responding in a helpful and compassionate manner. Maggie tried to assign those people to other jobs, but most ended up falling off the volunteer wagon. A conference room in the United Way Center was converted to serve as the case management war room. Eight computers and phones, which came to be busy ten hours a day, were installed. That was enough equipment. Much of a case manager's job was to visit clients at the site of their homes, and few case managers worked all day or every day.

Jack McCloud did a novel job of recruiting. He had to find men with some construction skills who were not regularly employed. He found one guy who could pound a nail straight at the county jail. He had two months remaining on work release and stayed on the team afterwards for the full run of the recovery. At $28 an hour, this was the best job he had ever had. Last I heard, he had used the recovery work to turn his life around. The experience enabled him to create a resume and find a job out of state.

Another recruit was a 28-year-old Dartmouth graduate who had rejected what he called the bullshit of the business world and was out of work. He clearly preferred to work with his hands rather than use his Ivy League education. He was about 6-2 and 220, in perfect shape, and could bench press 400 pounds. He too moved on after the recovery and combined his mind and body to start his own construction business in Missouri.

Among the other members of the team were a drywall-finishing specialist and a fireman whose avocation was carpentry. He could work only two days out of every three because he was on duty at the firehouse for 24 hours every third day. A painter and a retired carpenter rounded out the team. Although most of the men had specialties, everyone served, to some degree, as a generalist as well as a goodwill ambassador. I couldn't believe how many of these guys got invited to birthday parties and family dinners of the people whose homes they repaired. The only paid tradesman we used was a self-employed electrician who carved out time to fit us in as needed. He gave a discounted rate to all flood recovery jobs.

We learned that some national volunteer organizations concentrate on early response work in disasters while others specialize in recovery efforts. Still others work on the transition between the two steps. One such group was the Christian Reform World Recovery Committee or, as we called them, the Green Shirts. They came to town seventeen strong in mid-August and stayed for two weeks. Their specialty was outreach. They searched for victims who had yet not been helped. It was hard to believe how many people they found who didn't know about us. Despite the fact that the work of the Flood Recovery Team had been highly publicized and had been the subject of a high volume of word-of-mouth, some weren't aware of our existence and the help that was available. Others were embarrassed to ask for help, thinking of it as welfare. Still others were distrustful of all organized efforts that might be connected to government or big business.

The Green Shirts worked long days, knocking at the door of every home that had been affected. If the residents weren't home, they left a note instructing them to call the recovery office. If it appeared that the residents had left the home either temporarily or permanently, the Green Shirts asked neighbors how they might be reached, and they followed up. This group discovered about a hundred individuals and families who were not in our case files, most of whom were subsequently assisted by our team.

An estimated 2,200 homes were damaged to some degree. There were a variety of dispositions of those cases. Some experienced only minor damage, and the owners paid for the repairs without seeking help. For some, the FEMA money and SBA loan they received covered their cost, so we didn't hear from them. A few had flood insurance, which they used, and they were not visible to us. By the time those dispositions had occurred, we were down to about 550 cases that our team officially handled. There were also an undetermined number of others for whom our case managers facilitated the connection with FEMA, SBA, or their insurance company. Those instances were not counted in our case load records.

The construction team divided the homes that needed external and/or internal structural work into four categories. Total rebuilds meant tearing down the remains and keeping only the original foundation. For those, we built a new home. In fact in two cases, we couldn't even save the foundations. There were eight homes that qualified in that area. Major damage included houses that would require $20,000 or more to restore. Eighteen homes were in this category. Twenty-five homes made up the segment that was characterized as moderate damage—$5,000 to $20,000.

Of course, the largest category was those with minor damage—under $5,000. There were several hundred residences falling into this segment, including over a two hundred mobile homes. Almost all of the mobile homes needed to have the skirting replaced. Beyond that, the work was often minimal—little more than replacing drywall and some or all of the flooring. In addition, almost all of these places needed furniture.

Volunteers were a mixed blessing to our construction crew. Sometimes locals, usually parishioners from the victim's church, just showed up and offered to help with construction. In construction knowledge, these people ranged from having much experience to little experience to those who didn't know which end of the hammer to hold. The majority tended to be toward the low end of the continuum. Even the experienced ones often had a different way of doing things than our team. And many thought they knew how to do something that they really were not equipped to do. As was pointed out to me several times, hanging drywall is a relatively simple task that can be done by someone with a small amount of mechanical ability. But finishing drywall is a craft in itself. In addition, the volunteers that showed up one day and took our guys' time to give them instructions, often didn't come back.

All of this led to a generalization expressed by Jack McCloud in virtually every management team meeting, "Keep those fucking volunteers away from us so we can do our jobs." Maggie got the message and learned to screen those who specifically wanted to do construction and guide them to other jobs that required less expertise while still making them feel valued. That is a skill in itself which requires firmness coupled with diplomacy. She got to be very good at it.

The management team determined that our practice would be to give the benefit of the doubt as to victims' accounts of what they lost and other circumstances around their flood experience. Sierra County had $1.7 million from the Lilly grant through IAUW and another $300,000 from many individual and corporate contributions, a concert, and the local community foundation. We thought that would be enough to fund everything that needed to be done, but we didn't know what problems might pop up as we proceeded. Some caution needed to be exercised rather than simply our being a source for free money. A few people used their FEMA money to pay off their mortgages and then sought help from Long Term Recovery. This might appear to be wise money management, but it does not fit within the spirit of the work, not to mention the letter of the rules. It was never intended that the flood would provide home owners a windfall, after which they would be debt free and significantly better off than they had been before the flood. There were other instances where, when the case manager or construction crew went to the home, they saw a brand new pickup truck in the driveway or a new 60-inch plasma television in the living room. Sherry investigated these cases and generally ended up withholding money from those people.

Then there were the gray areas. In a few cases, Jack's crew found homes in such a state of disrepair that it was obvious that, while the flood had done some of the damage, the house had been a wreck before June. What do you do? We couldn't fix just the part that was affected by the flood. The choices were to fix it all or nothing. These cases were brought before the management team to determine if any of us had additional information about the case. Unless we had a compelling reason to refuse, we always decided to fix it all, and the flood just turned out to be a break for the owner. In my cynicism, I guessed that, within a year, the owner would allow the house to go to hell again. I never went back to check.

By early September, some people were getting back into their homes. It was time to address other losses. As I mentioned earlier, everything that was porous and had gotten wet had to be thrown away. This included furniture, carpet, clothing, wall board and often flooring and framing. The construction crew took care of the permanent building components, but someone else had to deal with furniture, clothing, and other household items that had been destroyed. Since we were committed to leaving victims at least as well of as they were before the flood, it was incumbent on Long-Term Recovery to provide replacements.

The homes we were working with were, for the most part, owned by citizens with low to moderate incomes. They didn't lose expensive furniture or designer clothes, but what they lost had been the best they could afford.

Often their losses consisted of furniture that was beaten up from years of use and clothing that was threadbare or patched. The management team declared that there wasn't enough decent used clothing or furniture available at second-hand stores to outfit several hundred families. We also decided that, within reason, we would take people's word as to what they had lost. And we took a *what-the-hell* position regarding victims ending up with new furniture when what they had lost was old. After what they had been through, Long Term Recovery was not going to be a cheapskate.

I felt that, if possible, buying from locally-owned retailers was important. I went to the best known mid-priced furniture store in town to meet with the owner. He was elderly, and he and I had never met. I told him what we were doing and offered him the opportunity to be our primary supplier of replacement furniture. I explained the potential of the business and asked if he could give some discount for these sales. I told him that we didn't want his entire profit, but if he could give 10%, it would be appreciated. Mostly, I just wanted a gesture of good faith. The owner refused to give any discount and obviously did not believe the scope of the business he might receive. I left determined to give him no flood recovery business. This is another instance of my lack of patience when it appears that people don't believe that I am acting in the best interest of others.

When I approached the owner of the next affordable store, whom I had also never met, I was met with similar doubt. I had my Flood Recovery Team shirt on, and I gave him my card identifying me as president of United Way, but I had no real credentials that showed my authority to make a deal. I explained that we were going to send flood victims to him to pick out whatever they wanted for up to three rooms at $1,300 per room. If more than three rooms of furniture at a single location had to be replaced, the limit was still $3,900 unless one of our soft-hearted case managers issued a waiver. The home-owner simply had to present a voucher issued by her case manager, choose her furniture, and drive off with it. The voucher stated how many rooms each person was eligible for. In cases where the recipient of the furniture absolutely could not pick up the furniture, the dealer agreed to deliver it at no charge. He also agreed to a 10% discount for all flood related purchases. Before it was over, the store had grossed over $300,000. Given typical furniture markups, I would guess that yielded a profit of around $100,000.

The case managers had access to a special fund that was set aside to purchase other replacement needs. They were authorized to grant up to $500 to buy kitchen items, clothing, lamps, tools, and other needs. A few families needed lawnmowers and garden implements. A larger grant had to be approved by Sherry, but there were only a few such requests. None of the case managers saw much attempted abuse of this system, and most recipients were extremely grateful.

By the time we reached July of 2009 (a year after the flood), the nurses had been called back to the hospital. Volunteering by many had run its course. I negotiated with the hospital to keep Sherry through the year. Her manager agreed on the condition that Long Term Recovery would pick up the cost of her salary and benefits. By that time, I could see that there was enough money to finish the job, so I was able to make that concession. There were still six case managers working who were committed to their clients. The case load had shrunk from a high of 550 to about 90, and this was manageable by the remaining team. Most of the low-hanging fruit related to construction had been picked, and most of the remaining work was on complete rebuilds and major repairs. This allowed the crew, which was still intact, to work more efficiently. Jack and his team could concentrate on a single job for a whole day or string of days without jumping around from job to job.

In mid-February 2010, the construction team pounded its last nail, and all cases were closed. A job that experts estimated would take three years was completed in twenty months. The end of a long **MACHETE MOMENT.**

## Charlie Dickens Was Right—the Best of Times and the Worst of Times Can Happen in the Same Era

*The Best:* The recovery effort received a small windfall in September after the flood. The A & E television network was producing a series of shows that took celebrities back to their roots. John Mellencamp is from Seymour, Indiana, just a few miles from Vienna. At the beginning of his career in 1976, when he still called himself Johnny Cougar and was unknown on the national stage, he played a concert at a 600-seat downtown theater in Vienna. I remember that my older son, who was eleven at the time, spent five dollars to attend. A & E decided that they would tape the show featuring Mellencamp at this theater, which had been closed for ten years. The civic group that owned the theater worked day and night for a week to install missing seats and to give the place a much-needed cleaning.

Mellencamp's management connections had heard about the flood and decided to contribute all proceeds to the flood recovery. However, admission was to be free, so we had to figure a way to create some proceeds. Tickets for the entire lower floor were to go to Mellencamp's family and hometown friends, A & E people, and other chosen guests. There were 150 seats in the balcony, and they gave all of those to the Flood Recovery Team to distribute as we saw fit. I called the steering committee together to decide how to glean income from the tickets. One of the pastors thought that maybe tickets could be sold for $50 each. Another was worried that we couldn't get that much and would be stuck with many of them. These guys had no idea as to what a big event this was or of the going price for concerts. To see a major rock star in a 600 seat room was unheard of. Mellencamp plays stadiums.

We finally decided that there would be a silent auction for pairs of tickets. Minimum bid would be $200 a pair, and the top 75 bidders would get two tickets each. Bids were to be dropped off at United Way Center by the Friday before the Tuesday concert. When bidding closed, there were over 300 checks covering bids for pairs of tickets. They ranged from the $200 minimum to $1,500. The concert raised $44,000, an average of $586 a pair with the low winning bid $381.

Kate and I were the balcony ushers for the event. We went in early and found that John was on stage playing acoustic guitar and singing some his better songs. We were delighted when he asked us if we could hear okay in the balcony. His connections from New York and Los Angeles, who were also in the theater early, could not have been nicer to work with. I had talked with them several times on the phone to establish our part of the arrangements. They went out of their way to come to the balcony to introduce themselves and to empathize with us about the flood and the recovery job. I even did an interview with a reporter from the Los Angeles Times, who was travelling from town to town following the A & E project. It was a highlight to do some good and have a tiny brush with celebrity.

The room was electric before and during the concert, and John and his band fed off of the crowd. No one sat for even a moment during the two-hour event with no break. Many in the balcony who were now successful professionals and community leaders had been teenagers in the seventies and eighties and were uninhibited in turning their personal clocks back to those halcyon days.

The **worst** didn't happen until a year after the recovery was completed. The community had succeeded in rebuilding homes and helping most of the flood victims to a life at least as good as before the flood. And we had done it in record time. All of us, both staff and volunteers, were basking in the glow of success. We had been selfless in helping our neighbors who were in trouble.

It turned out that there was one memorable exception to my positive observation. In the spring of 2011, just over a year after we finished, Jack McCloud walked out to his front lawn and shot himself. In his house, all of his possessions were divided into piles, each labeled as to which friend or relative was to be given those items.

As we reconstructed the final years of Jack's life, we learned that several people who knew him had suspected that he was depressed before the flood. Some had even confronted him and advised him to seek help. He hadn't worked since the flood and appeared to have spent his savings for day-to-day living. All agreed that his spirits rose as he got into the flood recovery work. He had something to be proud of—a reason to live. I remember that he took three or four of the tee shirts and wore one of them every day. I even ran into him around town a couple of times on weekends, and he had one on. Apparently, once the flood construction was over, he slipped back into his funk. At his funeral, we all debated what each of us could have done to prevent his final action, but we really didn't come up with any answers. Most agreed that had it not been for the flood, he might have acted two years earlier. Who knows?

# Out of the Frying Pan and into...

Although the flood work was winding down toward the end of 2009, I was not able to return to my routine United Way duties. Another event occurred that overlapped the flood recovery by two months. On Christmas

Eve 2009, the main building of the United Way Center was the site of a $5,000,000 fire. I was called about 8 PM, just as Kate and I were packing to catch a morning plane to visit our kids and grandkids for the holidays. I was told that a fire alarm had gone off in the building. It would not have been the first time the alarm had malfunctioned and sent a false message to the fire department. I assumed that was what had happened, but wanting to do due diligence, I put my shoes on and drove in. I couldn't have been more wrong. When I got eight blocks away, I smelled the roof burning. I arrived to find every fire department in the county on site pumping 1500 gallons of water a minute onto the entire west half of the building. Flames were shooting thirty feet above the roof. Within an hour, a couple hundred people had gathered in the parking lot to watch the proceedings. The sight was spectacular. I had never experienced such a helpless feeling in my life.

The west half of the top floor of the 140,000 square foot building was engulfed in flames. The original section was built circa 1915 and had been added on to by Munsey six times, which made the layout quite convoluted. Because of their unfamiliarity with the corridors coupled with the intense heat of the fire, the fire chief called all of his men out of the building at nine o'clock. It had already been determined that no one was inside. I could not fault his decision. It was a terribly dangerous situation.

About 11 o'clock, television crews from Indianapolis and Louisville started arriving. All I could do was stand and watch and thank friends and board members for coming to me and commiserating. I also gave brief interviews to each of the television stations. I really didn't need for this to be my fifteen minutes of fame. After about three hours, a lieutenant in the fire department came to me to say that they thought they had it contained. That made sense because the flames were no longer visible. Five minutes later, the wind shifted to come from the east, and the fire was roaring again. They were still pumping water on it the day after Christmas—48 hours after I got the call.

We were fortunate in that, at 40 degrees, it was not a particularly cold winter night. I had left my cell phone at home, so Kate was not able to reach me. When I didn't come home in two hours, she drove in to see what was going on. She knew it was bad when she had to walk the last four blocks because the police had blocked all the streets around the property.

She volunteered for the task of calling the kids to tell them we wouldn't be there for Christmas. She reported that, as we expected, they were great. They offered to fly in to help as soon as they could get a flight. I called them back and convinced them that there was nothing they could do, and their responsibility was to make a happy Christmas for their kids. I asked them to tell the grandchildren that Grandma and Grandpa loved them and would visit in January. Actually, it turned out to be February, but we made good on the promise.

The manager and board members of the GSC store, across the parking lot and out of harm's way, were terrific during and for two months after the fire. As the crowd dissipated to go home and prepare to celebrate Christmas, most of those who had a stake in the game stayed. The GSC folks invited us to use the store as a makeshift headquarters. They made coffee and brought in White Castle hamburgers. There's nothing like a half-dozen White Castles to comfort a man as he watches his life go up in smoke. We brought chairs and a couch from the furniture showroom to the front of the store. That gave us a warm vantage point from which to watch the proceedings. Kate and I and a few others hung there until about two o'clock when the lieutenant came in to tell us that it was going to be a long process, with nothing new was likely to happen soon and that we should go home.

Not having slept much, I arrived back on the scene about 6:30 Christmas morning. Santa Claus had not yet delivered to United Way Center. The lieutenant had been right. Nothing dramatic had taken place in my absence. My first job was to find locations where each of the displaced agencies could operate temporarily. There were 28 tenant agencies at that time, all of which needed a place to go. But it was Christmas Day. No prospects to supply space were available. I realized I had to wait twenty-four hours before I started begging.

I had a friend who was part of the public school administration. Their building was two blocks from United Way Center, and he had access. The members of the United Way staff who were in town and I spent the morning contacting agency leaders to invite them to a meeting at the school administration building at 1 o'clock on Christmas day. Amazingly, about twenty of the agencies were there, represented either by the executive director or a board member.

I knew that the agency representatives would have about a million questions. I tried to preempt most of them with my opening remarks. I told them that the fire was still burning and that no one would be able to enter the building for days. (That turned out to be almost two weeks.) I also shared with them my realization that if agencies were allowed to scatter and make commitments to new landlords, the co-location concept from which they and their clients had all benefitted would be dead forever. Therefore, I committed to working with them to find places for them to do business until we could rebuild. Of course, I had no idea whether I could keep that promise, but this was no time to show doubt. I figured we could make it work. I also invited them and anyone else in the community who was interested in our plight to a New Year's Eve grand reopening a year and six days hence. No one believed me, but they all humored me and said that if it happened, they would be there. I thought that having an imaginary light at the end of the tunnel would help to keep us focused.

I told them that there was nothing they could do today and that they should go home and enjoy Christmas with people they love. I then answered a few questions mostly with, "I don't know yet." I promised to send email updates at least daily and possibly every few hours in the first days. They should not be surprised if they were called to another meeting in two or three days. Most said that their staffs could work from home and use their cell phones for a few days, but they needed a place to go on January 2.

The next few days were chaos. GSC gave our crew two small offices and a drafty hallway to set up a headquarters and allowed us to use their break room for meetings. I spent the days and evenings of December 26 and 27 calling the owners of every empty office building, storefront, and warehouse in town to ask them to donate space for at least a couple of weeks and up to a year if possible. This job was made easier by several building owners calling me to offer space for one or more agencies. As with the flood, the outpouring of generosity was overwhelming.

By the second day, there were staff and volunteers totaling twelve people who would be working on a regular basis. I took the office next to the front door. The first couple weeks were really cold and windy, and every time the door opened, I got a blast of frigid wind. The rest of our team shared the slightly larger adjoining office and the drafty corridor. The space was wide enough to support tables used as desks without blocking traffic. I'm not sure that OSHA would have approved of the arrangement, but no one was going to ask them. The week between Christmas and New Year's yielded a constant flow of investigators. In addition to the FBI, there were local and state fire officials, several insurance company investigators, and various others.

Maggie had previously worked in the insurance business and understood the procedures and the jargon. She volunteered to handle the insurance people while I dealt with all of the other parties. The local fire marshal held the hammer as to when any of us would be allowed into the building. I assumed that, as the representative of ownership, I could go in as soon as the fire was out. WRONG! It was a week before any staff members were allowed in, and then it was on a very selective basis.

Fire officials, who surveyed the damage, gave periodic unofficial reports. The entire west half of the top floor was burned and was a total loss. The interior walls and the roof of that section were gone. File cabinets were melted, and all papers were destroyed. The floors, however, survived, having been built of such sturdy materials that the fire didn't penetrate them. (They don't build 'em like they used to.) The first floor was salvageable although none of the furniture and fixtures would be usable. There had been a freight elevator in the west end of the building that had been installed about 1930. It had let go and had fallen to the bottom of the shaft. The basement was filled with six feet of a mixture of water and hydraulic fluid from the aforementioned elevator. No part of the east half of the building experienced any fire damage. However, smoke and water had turned all of the contents into scrap. Throughout every floor of the building what hadn't been burned was ruined by smoke and water. Eventually, the entire building had to be gutted. Nothing remained except the outer walls, supporting I-beams, and a few internal concrete block weight bearing walls.

In my mind, we were going to raze the ruins of the west half of the top floor and put a roof over the second floor. That meant we would lose 20,000 of 80,000 rentable square feet. By then, Gallagher Brothers, Inc., a demolition and cleaning company from Chicago, was on the job. On December 28, I met with one of the brothers who owned the business and got a good feeling that his company would be reliable. One other such company contacted me that first week, but its representative did not strike me as particularly professional. A few others called after New Year, but they were too late.

I went to the mayor to request that the city waive the landfill charges. I don't know how many loads went there, but the dumpsters were filled with all of the furniture that had been in the building, all of the drywall, and all of the paper that could not be saved. His cooperation saved the United Way Center many thousand dollars.

In that first week, we really scrambled to find temporary space for agencies. I also learned of a few defections. The agencies operated by the state, welfare and child welfare, departed immediately and gave me to understand that they would make a permanent deal elsewhere, which they did. Although the center had lost its biggest tenant in both square feet and revenue, I felt okay about it. Coincidentally, they occupied about 20,000 square feet, which was the size of the area that burned irreparably. The state had been extremely difficult to work with. They were unreasonably demanding and rarely paid their rent on time, sometimes running as much as four months late. An interesting footnote: As little attention as they paid to ensuring their payments were timely, they sent a certified letter, dated December 28, to demand a refund of the seven days rent during which they could not occupy their space. And they gave us ten days to pay it. I paid it when it was convenient, which I think was in June.

Another interesting note about the two state operated agencies. Child welfare settled in a strip mall next door to a liquor store west of town. This is an agency that hosts supervised meetings of children and their parents who are such bad parents that their children have been taken away from them. Instead of enabling one-stop opportunities for those parents and children to access other necessary services at United Way Center, they now provide a location where those parents can see their kids and, in one stop, can buy their booze, cigarettes, and lottery tickets.

Working with the building owners that volunteered temporary space and those that were solicited, we found adequate space for fourteen of the displaced agencies that first week. Six, the two state agencies and four small ones, said they were going to move out permanently. The only time they were seen again was after the building was released by the fire marshal and they could go in and redeem any items that could be saved. Three others found temporary space on their own but said they wanted to return if the United Way Center was rebuilt—a decision that had been made only in my mind. Two agencies said that their staffs could work from home for a while.

For the domestic violence prevention agency, we were able to leverage off the flood recovery. The hospital had bought a pair of double-wide mobile homes and put them on the grounds to use as offices during the flood recovery. They provided those two structures indefinitely, which turned out to be a year. That left us two agencies to place, which we accomplished the first week of the New Year.

The locations varied. One moved in with the Girl Scouts office in the fire house building on our campus directly across the street from the main building. The local CEO of the electric company, who happened to be on our board, called to offer a building on his property that was going to be open for a year. One of our larger agencies moved into that building. Two sizable agencies moved to warehouses that also contained offices. The others were scattered among empty store fronts, an unused room in a law offices, and a closed factory. The problem that remained was that only the hospital, electric company, and the Girl Scouts spaces were going to be available for the full year. The others could commit for only a couple of months.

Then there was another example of generosity. My buddy Trish at the Denard Foundation was aware of two large buildings owned by Denard that were vacant at the moment. Both were on the edge of the downtown area about a mile from each other. One was a one-story office building of about 10,000 square feet. The other was another product of the flood. It had been occupied before it was buried in the flood waters. The Denard people who worked there had been moved to another facility, and it was decided that they would stay there permanently. The company's revised plan was to clean up after the flood, a project they were just completing, and use the building to house production of a new product line. As luck would have it, that 40,000 square feet of factory space would sit empty for a year because Denard officials had delayed the startup. That meant the building would be empty for all of 2010, and we could use it. I had to promise to be out by January 1, 2011. Few believed that promise, but I made it anyway. I was already hanging out with so many commitments of which I was uncertain that I thought one more wouldn't hurt.

Trish personally went to every member of the Denard operating committee to get them to sign off on loaning us the two buildings so that the co-location could be held together. As soon as the deal was definite, I took the agency leaders on a tour of the buildings. I assigned the ones that absolutely needed the privacy of separate offices to the smaller building, which was already divided into many private offices. The agencies that were too large for that building or could get by with cubicles were offered space in the larger building. Some of them whined that they could not work without the privacy of closed offices, but when it was that or nothing, they adapted. I contend that the need for confidentiality, while crucial for some, is way overstated in the human services industry.

United Way Center did not have to pay for the space, but it was responsible for cleaning and other minor maintenance. To cover that, we charged the tenants 20% of what they had paid before the fire with a minimum of $100 a month. Denard allowed me to design the layout to fit the needs of each agency. I did that in consultation with each of the tenants. Then Denard maintenance employees assembled the cubicles, attached the desk tops, and brought in whatever other furniture was necessary for the agencies to operate It didn't all match, but no one cared. The smaller of the Denard buildings was available immediately, and the agencies going there moved in within a week. The larger space was ready for occupancy by mid-February. In keeping with their practice of generosity, Denard supplied the manpower and equipment to move everyone in.

We worked it out that everyone could stay in their short-term digs until we were all able to move to the Denard space. The agencies that moved to the Girl Scouts office, the double-wides, and the electric company were able to stay put at those locations for the entire year.

Meanwhile, Groundhog Day came and went, and the staff and volunteers were still in the cold of the GSC store and were damn happy to have it. By mid-January, the fire department was out of the picture except when they were needed by the insurance investigators. They had already determined that there was no one at fault for the fire. While they never found the exact location of the problem, they were convinced that it was caused by faulty sixty-year-old wiring. The cleanup was underway by the Gallagher crew and a cadre of volunteers and staff members of the agencies. The agency people stuck to their own areas, packing up what was salvageable and taking the rest to the dumpster. A few agencies hired an organization that specializes in restoring paper that has been damaged. United Way didn't have much that was salvageable, but Kate and another volunteer did what they could by hanging wet paper on a clothesline to dry. Then they made copies of the dry pieces that were legible. Talk about a low-tech process! But it worked.

You can imagine the kind of men Gallagher hired to carry out damaged furniture and knock down walls. They had a crew of about twenty, and I would guess that fifteen of them weighed upwards of 240 with little fat on them. And all of them had an impeccable work ethic. The sheriff furnished a half-dozen work release prisoners—the ones with the bracelets on their ankles--to help with cleanup. Their work ethic was less impeccable (do we call that peccible?), and we sent them back to jail after a few days.

The United Way staff integrated the Gallagher guys into our activities. About once a week, the staff invited them for pizza or chicken or a pitch-in in the GSC break room, and several times, we joined them at a local blue collar bar from which they could walk to their hotel. I made it to as many of the gatherings as I could fit into my schedule. I've been with my share of hard-drinking groups, and these guys could hold their own with any of them. But they were fun to be with. They were genial, funny, and generous, and the servers loved them because of their tendency to tip wildly.

Here's an example of how a board of directors can have no clue and how they can jeopardize or at least slow actions that obviously need to be performed. I was prepared to spend the February board meeting discussing plans to rebuild, including choosing a general contractor and getting some idea of what the new building would look like. To me, it was a no-brainer that United Way Center would be rebuilt. One board member, Jules Farrell, who slowed every meeting by repeating his same point over and over, started the ball rolling by asking whether we should rebuild. I guess the alternative would have been to take the money and run, which would have left the twenty-some agencies that I had promised could come back in a year, out in the cold. Of course, I was criticized for making that promise, because I did not have the authority to do so. MORE BULLSHIT!

Once Jules made his comments, other board members jumped in. It was like a brush fire. It was a short leap to the suggestion that we look at other sites for the co-location, even though there was not one empty building in town larger than 25,000 square feet. The current location was perfect. It was on the bus line in the center of the city and county and was near the part of town where most of the lower income people tended to live. By the end of the meeting, I had been given an assignment to research these questions and report back at the March board meeting. What a waste of time! The staff and I had been working twelve hours a day, seven days a week, trying to manage United Way and keep the tenant agencies together. The board called it due diligence; I call it needless barrier building. I know the cliche that says there are no dumb questions, but these were dumb questions.

I carried out the assignment, but without asking permission, I preempted the board's decision by soliciting bids from the four largest contractors in the county. This wasn't met with glee when the board found out what I did, but it got everyone back into the building a month sooner than if I had waited.

Actually, Jules is not a bad guy. He is well intended, amiable, hard-working, and he walks the highest possible moral ground. He can be interesting and even funny when talking about subjects away from my job. He's good to drink a beer with. He's just a pain in the ass as a board member.

This shows what can happen when boards want to control activities without realizing the ramifications of their actions. If I had followed their instructions, all of the agencies would have been displaced for an extra month, and Denard would not have gotten its building back by the promised date. We would have been the cause of Denard's having to delay introduction of a new product line. Not to mention that my New Year's Eve party would never have happened.

The contract was awarded to Lund Construction. After meeting with Lund engineers, the decision was made to raze the west half of the second floor and cover it with a new roof. We asked the Gallaghers to complete that portion of the demolition first. That allowed Lund to put a roof over the first floor of that section of the building before the weather caused more damage. After cleaning and demolition were finished, the rest of the construction began the next day.

The Gallagher crew completed their cleanup in early April with the final step of drying the inside of the building. The bill was $1.4 million, or about a fourth of the insurance proceeds. It was well worth it, and it left us with a little over three-and-a-half million to rebuild. While the cleanup was ongoing, at the request of the Lund engineers, United Way Center hired a local architect, and he and I worked together on the internal design. As part of my role, I conferred with the tenants as to their desired configuration of their space. The larger agencies wanted private offices for most of their staff, so there had to be a meeting of the minds. I explained that every time a wall was built, the cost increased by several thousand dollars. Furthermore, the agencies had proven they could work in cubicles, because they had done it for a year. Finally, there was a series of compromises that reduced by half the number of private offices. That enabled us to replace many offices with clusters of cubicles.

The Lund project manager was Tom Colfax. Tom was an engineer out of Purdue and was not only extremely competent, he was also absolutely unflappable. I tried to hold change orders to a minimum, but I still asked a lot of questions and made quite a few requests. Tom remained flexible throughout the project. The board wanted to appoint a building committee that would meet weekly with Tom and me. This was one committee that actually added some value. A couple of members had a lot more experience and knowledge about buildings than I did and made several helpful observations and suggestions.

The Lund workers stayed on task. They were obviously committed to finishing by the deadline, and they made sure that the sub-contractors did the same. By the September board meeting, much of the construction was far enough along that I scheduled for us to meet in the space that would become the United Way offices. The flooring was just plywood, and the staff assembled a makeshift conference table out of sawhorses with plywood laid over them. This proved to be a symbolic moment. I believe that the spirits of the directors, many of whom were skeptical about the rebuild, were buoyed, and there was a sense that this thing was actually going to happen.

That same month, I decided to spread the enthusiasm by taking groups of tenant employees to walk through their areas. For each walk-through, the construction guys halted their work for a few minutes in each section we visited. The work was far from finished, but the agency staffers (mostly women who did not have a single hard-hat as part of their wardrobes) were thrilled to put on a hard-hat and go see where their new home was to be.

Six years earlier, Sara Quinlan, had worked for United Way as executive director of First Call for Help. She left when she was offered a job with IAUW as a liaison to the state legislature. About ten days after the fire, she walked into our temporary office at GSC. She announced that she was going to take time from her regular assignments at IAUW to work twenty hours a week to do whatever would be of value in our recovery. This was one of the best strokes of good fortune in this whole fiasco. Without being asked, Sara took on the task of soliciting donations of furniture. If she were to be successful, that would take the burden of that expense off the agencies. She made calls to furniture manufacturers and businesses across the country to solicit donations of office furniture and fixtures. I appreciated her offer, but I had no great expectations as to what her results would be.

In anticipation of some degree of success, I asked to borrow some space in a local warehouse that had about 5,000 square feet that the occupant wasn't using. Within a week, truckloads of furniture started to arrive. That space was filled in about three days, and I started making contacts in the hope of finding more. Before it was over, there was furniture stacked at four different locations. It came so fast that no one had time to keep an accurate inventory of what was where. It wasn't all new, but most was in good to excellent condition. Only a very small portion was junk. Much of the furniture was from the offices of businesses that were remodeling or had recently done so. Their old furniture was expendable, and they figured this was a good use for it. Denard gave us the cubicles and furniture we had used in its building. When it was time, their people installed them to our specifications. What would we have done without Denard?

Kimball Office Furniture, a manufacturer in Jasper, Indiana, sent enough high-end discontinued models of executive furniture to fill fifteen offices. It was still in the original crates. I decided to distribute that among the executive directors of various agencies. Those folks are not paid nearly enough, and I thought this would be a nice perk. As United Way president, I took one set for myself. There were a desk, a long credenza, and equally long over-hanging storage in each set. I checked the Kimball catalogue and found out that there was over $20,000 worth of furniture in my office. That is not normal in the human services business.

The final outcome of Sara's work was that no agency had to buy one stick of furniture when it moved back in. Because of the lack of inventory control, each organization was asked to list their needs by category such as 12 desks and chairs, 6 lateral files, 20 side chairs, etc. In filling the orders, I made sure that everyone got some excellent and some good items.

In November, the city code enforcement officer reluctantly allowed full use of the loading dock and our 15,000 square foot warehouse area, which had high ceilings. A local moving company was contracted to bring everything from the outlying locations into the warehouse area of United Way Center. The warehouse was stacked to the ceiling with free furniture. After we were granted occupancy, the movers were brought back the first week of January. They delivered all of the furniture from the warehouse to the offices, where it will live out its useful days.

The final days of construction were dedicated to finishing touches. On December 30 at 5 PM, the code enforcement officer approved the building for occupancy on the condition that the list of items he required, none of which were safety issues, would be completed within a month. He said he didn't want to endure my wrath by ruining my New Year's Eve. In fact, he and his wife would be there on their way to another party.

Continuing our string of good fortune, Tom Colfax had a garage band that played 50's and 60's rock and roll. For the party, they stationed themselves in the lobby next to the entrance. The entire community had been invited to the grand opening, which was to take place from 5 to 7 o'clock so that it didn't interfere with other holiday plans. About 400 citizens toured the building, had cookies and punchless punch, and were overwhelmed by the quality of the new United Way Center. All agreed that it was much better than before the fire. My last and possibly most gratifying work related **MACHETE MOMENT.**

# VII.

# THE WRAPUP

After a thoroughly enjoyable and productive career at United Way, it was unfortunate that my later years had to be confusing for me. Maybe it's an age thing. The rules changed, and nobody told me. I had had virtually free rein in decision making for fourteen years. Our board chairs had been a succession of CEO's of large and small companies in the community. I had hand-picked every one of them. Then, somehow that privilege got away from me. In those final years, there were people who were department heads or individual contributors for their respective employers.

I was no longer considered the expert. The new chairs created committees to study every issue that I had traditionally decided. This reduced my ability to create and respond quickly and with flexibility. At that point, I felt that we had a grinding process that sometimes produced untimely and mediocre results. We went from quick decisions, about which I kept the board apprised, to a requirement of my asking the board's permission before I acted or spoke. They even wanted to wordsmith my guest opinion articles in the newspaper, which I had produced two or three times every year. These articles had been well received and were effective in keeping the community informed on important issues. Except for when I broke their rules, which I did often enough for some board members to label me a *loose cannon*, I felt like a toothless tiger. It's funny how the description of the same guy can go from visionary, leader, and man of action to loose cannon. Oh, well.

My conclusion is that it is almost impossible to judge the work of a CEO unless you've been one. Each of the three chairs I alluded to had a single responsibility in his/her day job. None of them had ever had an experience to learn what it's like to have responsibility for everything—operations, sales, finance, customer service, media and community relations, quality, delivery, legal requirements, and whatever else fit within Harry Truman's declaration, "The buck stops here."

I blame myself for this creeping deterioration of authority. Part of it is my adherence to my philosophy item 3—trust. I didn't realize the difference between being trustful and being naive. At our United Way, about 20% of the board turns over, and there is a new chair every year. Some non-profit organizations have two year terms, but seldom is it more than that. Every time there was a change of board leadership, I should have renewed the understanding of my responsibilities and level of authority. Then, at least I would have known if the new board leaders disagreed with the traditional arrangement. By not gaining that assurance, the president's level of authority can disintegrate over time. He will wake up one day and find that the job is not the one he signed up for.

I wouldn't be so absolute in my thinking if the United Way of Sierra County had not enjoyed such great success in my first fourteen years of groundbreaking work and successful outcomes in times of crises. I can't even say with certainty that this wasn't a good time to make a change of leadership. It may have been that, just as it had been at Kane and Thursby, I had given all I had to give—no more dragons.

Without going into great detail, I will let it suffice to say that disagreements with board leaders became more frequent, and I got more frustrated and angry. The situation became untenable for both sides, and we agreed that I would retire at the annual meeting of 2012—almost seventeen years after I had started.

I would be remiss not to acknowledge many positive events that occurred during those final years. I also credit the staff for their great contributions to those many successes. I can also say that there were countless times when board members also made an undeniable difference.

- We conducted a record campaign in each of those years.
- The Annual Meeting of 2011 was held in a large unfinished area of our then three-month old rebuilt structure. It was quite well

attended, which gave many community and business leaders and donors the opportunity to see what had and had not been done to the building. (That 5,000 square foot unfinished space has since been built out and is rented and producing revenue.)

- At that meeting, I publicly gave a 52-week notice of my retirement. As the last agenda item of the day, it was announced that effective immediately the name of the United Way Center would be changed to the Joe Camarte Center. A carved stone 8 feet high and 16 feet long was placed in front of the main building to commemorate my service to United Way and the community. The same board with which I had been increasingly at odds for three years bestowed this unbelievable honor on me. Not only that—one of the two leaders of the movement to rename the property was Jules Farrell. Talk about mixed feelings! I have unforgettable resentment and tremendous gratitude toward the same twenty people. I've landed on the decision to forgive and be grateful.
- My official final day on the job was the Annual Meeting of 2012. I was given the last twenty minutes on the agenda to express my feelings about the past seventeen years. I stayed on the high ground, giving many thanks and sharing positive memories. I couldn't resist a plug for early child development as the most important issue to be dealt with. Finally, I delivered my own parody of Bob Hope's signature sign-off song, *Thanks for the Memories,* which I had written with great care over my final year. I left the podium to a standing ovation and have never tried to influence my successor's work.

A few months before my departure, it was necessary to recruit my successor. Of course, you know who stepped up to lead the search committee—Jules Farrell. I was not involved in the search in any way, which is how it should have been. I will say that Jules and his committee did an excellent and thorough job. After sifting through about 50 applications, they interviewed twelve candidates by phone. Then they conducted face-to-face interviews with six of those, and finally they made a choice from two finalists.

They got it right. They chose an intelligent young man in his early forties who lives in Vienna. He had several years of experience leading an agency in inner-city Indianapolis. Working in that neighborhood implies a significant amount of toughness and savvy. And he is conditioned to work more successfully than I ever could in terms of political correctness and the involvement of committees, task forces, focus groups, surveys, and outcome measurements—all that stuff that, for fifty years, I have referred to as bullshit. Bullshit or not, that's what life in the 21$^{st}$ century demands. It seems to me that every move has to be made with the thought in mind that your action could be the basis for litigation or severe criticism from people who don't understand the facts.

Who's right? Who knows? I had some success doing things my way, and hopefully the new generation will succeed despite what my old eyes see as self-created barriers. United Way is a superb organization and has many dedicated supporters, both here and across the country. Ours has an outstanding president and staff and a committed board. It will continue to make a huge difference to everyone—rich and poor—with or without me. I'm proud to have been a part in its success.

I stayed to manage the Joe Camarte Center on a half-time basis for a small salary and fully paid Medicare with the best supplemental health and prescription plans for both Kate and me. At this writing, I have just turned 72, and I'm truly happy working in my basement office at the JCC, going home to get my ass kicked in Scrabble on a regular basis by Kate, going to movies and out to dinner with her, and visiting our kids and grandkids as often as possible. In January, I suffered a stroke which hospitalized me for five days, but I'm well now. I tire more quickly than before, but I'm retraining myself to walk with a natural gait, and my speech is normal. I plan to be back on the tennis court within a couple of months.

It has been and still is a great life. I'm glad that I was able to work with each of my former employers. There were good and bad experiences with each, but the vast majority were good. As I look back, I feel neither beholden nor acrimonious toward the companies and the individuals I worked alongside. As far as I'm concerned, I'm even with the world. And every time I pass the rock in front of the main building, I get a warm feeling.

I have tried to identify which of my characteristics have contributed the most to my good luck, and I have come up with four:

1. At every crossroads, I consciously try to live by all of the tenets of my philosophy, even if doing so produces an unfavorable result for me.

2. I have, to some degree, better than average intelligence and vision. I'm not saying I'm the smartest guy in the room, but I usually have a pretty good understanding of areas in which I choose to participate.

3. I have no conflict between religious beliefs and logic. Some will consider this as contrary to number one on this list, but that is not the case. I see the Golden Rule as a secular guideline, not a religious one. I support people in following their chosen religion as long as their doing so doesn't affect me or my organization. I can point to an unbelievable number of elected leaders at all levels of government, from small-town mayors to governors to members of Congress and right on up to some of the past occupants of the White House, who say they turn to God as part of their decision making process. If they want to pray that they make the right decision, have at it. But if they think they talk to God or make some interpretation of the Bible to decide how they vote, they should not be in office. Using a vote arrived at in that manner on something that will affect others is unacceptable.

4. I have a gigantic set of balls. I have no fear of embarrassment over making a mistake. I said and did enough embarrassing things in my first fifty or so years to last a lifetime, so I decided that it wasn't productive to worry about that.

   There is a description often applied to people who choose to attain success by sucking up to those above them on the organization chart. It is said that they, "Kiss up and kick down." I prefer to do the opposite, "Kick up and kiss down."

   To say I kick up is a little extreme. I don't actually kick, but I also don't take everything high ranking people say as gospel. As I said in my philosophy Item 10, I see it as my duty to question authority. I believe that should be part of everyone's modus operandi. I told you the stories of my approaches to people in high positions—the CEO of Denard, Inc. about the Boy Scouts, the CEO of Munsey Industries to get the building donated, and the Senior VP of the

Commercial Bank of Charlotte as we were near bankruptcy. My approach to congressmen, mayors, business leaders, and chairs of my own board of directors has been consistent. I say it the way I see it and argue if they have a perspective that I don't agree with. Usually I do it respectfully. At the other end of the social and professional spectrum, I treat people in lesser jobs and those who are not well off with respect.

To reduce my career to numbers, I would say that I have had at least fifty joyful experiences to every downer. And if I had to single out one of the above characteristics as the most significant, I would have to say **BIG BALLS**.

Writing this has been fun, but I have to go now. My twin two-year-old granddaughters are waking up from their naps, and I have to go play Ring-Around-the-Rosie. The biggest of all **MACHETE MOMENTS**.